IMAGES
of America

FILIPINOS IN
WASHINGTON, D.C.

RECEPTION AND DANCE FOR THE LATE PRESIDENT RAMON MAGSAYSAY'S BIRTHDAY
Sponsored by the Filipino American Fraternity
Statler Hilton Hotel, Washington, D. C.   August 29, 1964
Guest Speaker Hon. Oscar Ledesma   Dr. John G. Udan, President
Hon. Co-Social Chairmen: Mrs. Hilariona Puyot and Mrs. Anastasia D. Salvoron

This book primarily covers the settlement and stories of Filipinos who arrived between 1900 and 1964. In the 1960s, U.S. Interstate 495, also known as the Capital Beltway—or simply, the beltway—was built, encircling Washington, D.C., and its inner suburbs. The beltway provides a metaphoric marker for the focus of this book: the arrival and settlement of Filipinos to Washington, D.C. The beltway was completed around 1964, improving the flow of traffic and mobility around Washington, D.C. In the above photograph, the Filipino American Fraternity hosts a dinner and dance at the Statler Hilton Hotel in Washington, D.C., on August 29, 1964. (Courtesy of the Cacas family.)

ON THE COVER: The Filipino Capitols and fans pose for a team picture. In an accompanying letter dated August 21, 1947, the team's representative, Francisco Solis, thanks his counterpart, Francisco Alayu, for hosting an athletic meet held in 1947 in Chicago, where several of their team's trophies are displayed. (Courtesy of Fran Alayu Womack, Chicago.)

IMAGES
of America

FILIPINOS IN
WASHINGTON, D.C.

Rita M. Cacas and Juanita Tamayo Lott

ARCADIA
PUBLISHING

Published by Arcadia Publishing
Charleston SC, Chicago IL, Portsmouth NH, San Francisco CA

Library of Congress Control Number: 2009925460

For all general information contact Arcadia Publishing at:
Telephone 843-853-2070
Fax 843-853-0044
E-mail sales@arcadiapublishing.com
For customer service and orders:
Toll-Free 1-888-313-2665

Visit us on the Internet at www.arcadiapublishing.com

*We honor the early 20th century pioneers who left
their homeland to build new lives, opening the way
for the next Washington, D.C., Filipinos.*

CONTENTS

ACKNOWLEDGMENTS

We extend our sincere thanks to enthusiastic D.C.-area contributors and supporters who gave generously of their family stories, albums, artifacts, and help during our community day events. Individuals include Gus Alzona; Sonia Aranza; Crisanto Basilio; Mary Buena; Remegio and Carolina Cabacar; Max, Sam, and Dora Cacas; Mendell Calabia; Christopher Shove Cook (who took many of the photographs in this book); Josefino and Diana Comiso; Rosario Curameng; Gem Daus; Emily Cacas Gonzales; Benjamin de Guzman; Emma Delarosa; Alex DePeralta Sr.; Maria DePeralta Ferrara; Kay, Leonardo, and Roy Fuñe; Margie Guerrero Wegmann; Mencie Hairston; Angela and Christina Lagdameo; Napoleon Lechoco; Lina Undayag McDowell; Flora Corpuz Nivera; Nila and Joe Straka; and Leo Toribio. In memory of the pioneers from Rita Cacas's 1993 photo documentary project, *A Visit with My Elders: Portraits and Stories of Washington, D.C. Filipinos,* we honor Fernando Aguilar, Leon and Ana Alcoy, Remegio Aqui, Tomas and Presentacion Banda, Bibiano Bitanga, Moises and Monica Bautista, Clemente Cacho Cacas, Florentina DePeralta, Patricio Guibao, Fidel Herrin, Juliana Panganiban, Matteo and Consuelo Perez, Peter Salmon, Cesario Savellano, Pedro Sarmiento, Januario and Hilariona Sevilla, and Rudolfo Zepeda.

We are grateful to organizations, longtime friends, and colleagues from Before the Beltway: Maria Cacas, Tino Calabia, Sandra and Lisa Sabino Chinn, Evangeline Abellera Paredes, Clavelina and Pedro Sarmiento, and Tony Sarmiento; Filipino American National Historical Society (FANHS): Joanie May Cordova, Dawn Mabalon, Mel Orpilla, and Fran Alayu Womack; National Archives and Records Administration: Nicholas Natanson and Steven Puglia; Smithsonian Institution, Asian Pacific American Program: Gina Inocencio, Charmaine Manansala, Franklin Odo, and Francey Lim Youngberg; University of Maryland in College Park, Maryland, Asian American Studies (AAST) Program: Larry Shinegawa, et al., and Asian American Studies-Filipino American Studies (FAST) Class: Gem Daus, et al., and research intern Rachel Parker; the Filipino Cultural Association, University of Maryland in College Park, Maryland; and the Organization of Young Filipino Americans, University of Virginia in Charlottesville, Virginia. There are names, faces, and stories that did not make it onto the pages of this book, but this is just a beginning. There are many more faces and stories of the D.C. area and East Coast Filipinos for Images of America. We await the rich histories about Filipinos of New York, Baltimore, Philadelphia, Virginia Beach, and others, ready to be told.

Our deepest appreciation goes to the Cacas Cook and Tamayo Lott families; especially to Maria Cacas and Vangie Paredes; and to our peer reviewers, Tony Sarmiento (past board member, Historical Society of Washington, D.C.) and Wendy Lim (author of *Chinatown, D.C., A Photographic Journal,* 1991).

INTRODUCTION

Filipinos in Washington, D.C. presents a compelling story of the establishment and progression of Filipinos in the nation's capital from 1900 to 1964. The story began with the United States's annexation of the Philippines, which allowed Filipinos to freely enter America as students, seamen, farm laborers, or soldiers. Filipinos fought alongside U.S. soldiers during World War II, and in 1946, the Philippines became independent from the United States. In the mid-1960s, U.S. immigration laws were reformed, opening the door to an influx of Filipino teachers, artists, scientists, and medical professionals into the United States.

Filipinos in Washington, D.C. captures an immigrant and ethnic history and documents historical events and political transitions that occurred inside the beltway, which had significant impact on the nation and the world in the middle of the 20th century. Completed in 1964, the beltway provides a metaphoric perimeter marking the early arrivals and the settlement of a permanent Washington, D.C., metropolitan-area Filipino community.

This book has long been in the making in the imagination of Rita Cacas. She and her siblings were born in Washington, D.C., and grew up in Oxon Hill, Maryland, in the 1950s, second-generation Filipino Americans. In 1929, their father, Clemente Cacho Cacas, arrived in the United States as the Great Depression began. After serving in World War II, he returned to the Philippines and brought his postwar bride, Maria Bello, to the United States in 1953. Clemente drove a Washington, D.C., taxicab for over 40 years and often brought one of the children with him on Saturdays to learn about the city and tell stories of places where Filipinos lived and socialized.

A professional photographer and archivist, Rita sought to acknowledge and thank her parents, aunts, uncles, and other pioneers who sacrificed for their children to achieve the American dream. With a grant from the Prince George's Arts Council in 1993, she conducted research and photographed some early Filipino Washington, D.C., settlers and captured their stories. Rita's work confirmed the existence of a long-established and thriving community in the Washington, D.C., area, culminating in a 1994 photograph-documentary collection of professionally produced photographic exhibits and a lecture entitled *A Visit with My Elders: Portraits and Stories of Washington area Filipino Pioneers*.

The exhibit's opening in 1994 at George Washington University's Colonnade Gallery was reported in the *Washington Post* by the Washington, D.C., chronicler Sarah Booth Conroy. Since then, the portraits have been displayed locally and nationally and stories shared with various audiences in local venues, federal government agencies, galleries, universities, and at the Smithsonian Institution's National Portrait Gallery. In 2006, a group of children of the pioneer generations began to meet informally to share stories of growing up in the city and its suburbs long before the construction of the Capital Beltway in 1964. From oldest to youngest, the children were Vangie Paredes, Pete Sarmiento, Lee Sarmiento, Maria Cacas, Tino Calabia, Sandy Sabino Chinn, Tony Sarmiento, Rita Cacas, and Lisa Chinn. The group became known as Before the Beltway, facilitated by Juanita Tamayo Lott, a 1973 transplant from the San Francisco Filipino American community.

Building upon Rita's work, the group shared stories and photographs, family memorabilia, going to school, socializing in a segregated capital, and being pioneers themselves as they entered mainstream America. They moved into careers in the federal government—both civilian and military—and other previously denied institutions of employment.

In a fall 2006 meeting of Before the Beltway, the first newly appointed permanent director of Asian American Studies Program at the University of Maryland, College Park (UMCP), Dr. Larry Shinagawa, attended. Larry and the group spoke about potential collaborations including the creation of Filipino American Studies at the university and a potential book about the Before the Beltway community. At the time, the first of Arcadia Publishing's Images of America series on Filipino Americans were released, such as Mel Orpilla's *Filipinos in Vallejo* (2005) and *San Francisco's Japantown* (The Japantown Task Force, Inc. , 2005)—about the San Francisco neighborhood that Juanita and her brother Bill Tamayo were raised in and attended elementary school. In July 2008, the Filipino American National Historical Society (FANHS) Conference in Anchorage, Alaska, featured workshops including *Filipinos in Hollywood* (Montoya, 2008), and *Filipinos in the East Bay* (Buell, et al., 2008).

In addition to preserving their families' pioneering efforts as Americans in Washington, D.C., Before the Beltway members were equally committed to passing on this legacy to younger, U.S.-born Filipino Americans and to new, post-1965 immigrants. In April 2007, the group partnered with the UMCP Asian American Studies Program (AAST) and the student organization Filipino Cultural Association (FCA) to launch the new Filipino American Studies (FAST) courses by hosting the first FAST gala. At the second studies gala in February 2009, this nucleus—in partnership with UMCP alumni and community members—launched the Major General Antonio Taguba Profiles in Courage and Leadership Scholarship to recognize and develop leaders for federal service, both military and civilian.

One

FROM U.S. NATIONALS TO CAPITAL COMMUNITIES

In 1898, after being a Spanish colony for over three centuries, Filipinos successfully rebelled. With Spain's defeat in the Spanish-American War, Filipinos fought against recolonization by the United States under Gen. Emilio Aguinaldo, who established a Philippine Republic in 1899. In 1901, American forces and weapons overpowered the Filipino revolutionaries, captured Aguinaldo, and the Philippines became a U.S. colony with a civilian governor under the U.S. Bureau of Insular Affairs. The photograph above documents the New Year's Eve celebration of three local Filipino organizations composed of U.S. nationals in 1938: the Visayan Circle, Inc; the Rising Boholanos, Inc.; and the Filipino Club, Inc. (Courtesy of the Toribio family.)

9

In 1900, Washington, D.C., was the center of discussion about the future of the new U.S. colony as President McKinley appointed members of the Philippine Commission. In this photograph are Luke E. Wright of Tennessee; Henry C. Ide of Vermont; chairman William H. Taft; Prof. Bernard Moses of California; and Prof. Dean C. Worcester of Michigan. Their counterparts in the Philippines were elected Filipino representatives to the National Assembly to work with the Philippine Commission. After passage of the Jones Act in 1916, which formally declared U.S. commitment to grant Philippine independence, the Filipino people, via the National Assembly and the Philippine Legislature, were given full control over legislative affairs. The American governor-general, however, retained the right to veto. Filipinos became American subjects known as U.S. nationals. (Courtesy of the National Archives and Records Administration.)

To prepare the Philippines for eventual independence, the United States established a civil government during its occupation of the country. A rich variety of records documenting the period of American occupation are available at the U.S. National Archives in Washington, D.C. One example of records available at the National Archives is covered by Record Group (RG) 350, the Bureau of Insular Affairs, whose main function was to administer the customs and supervise the civil affairs of territories acquired by the United States in the Spanish-American War. These records cover American government operations in the Philippine Islands (1898–1939), Puerto Rico (1898–1900 and 1909–1934), and Cuba (1898–1902). This photograph (from RG 350) shows a group of military officials sent to the Philippines during the American occupation. (Courtesy of the National Archives and Records Administration.)

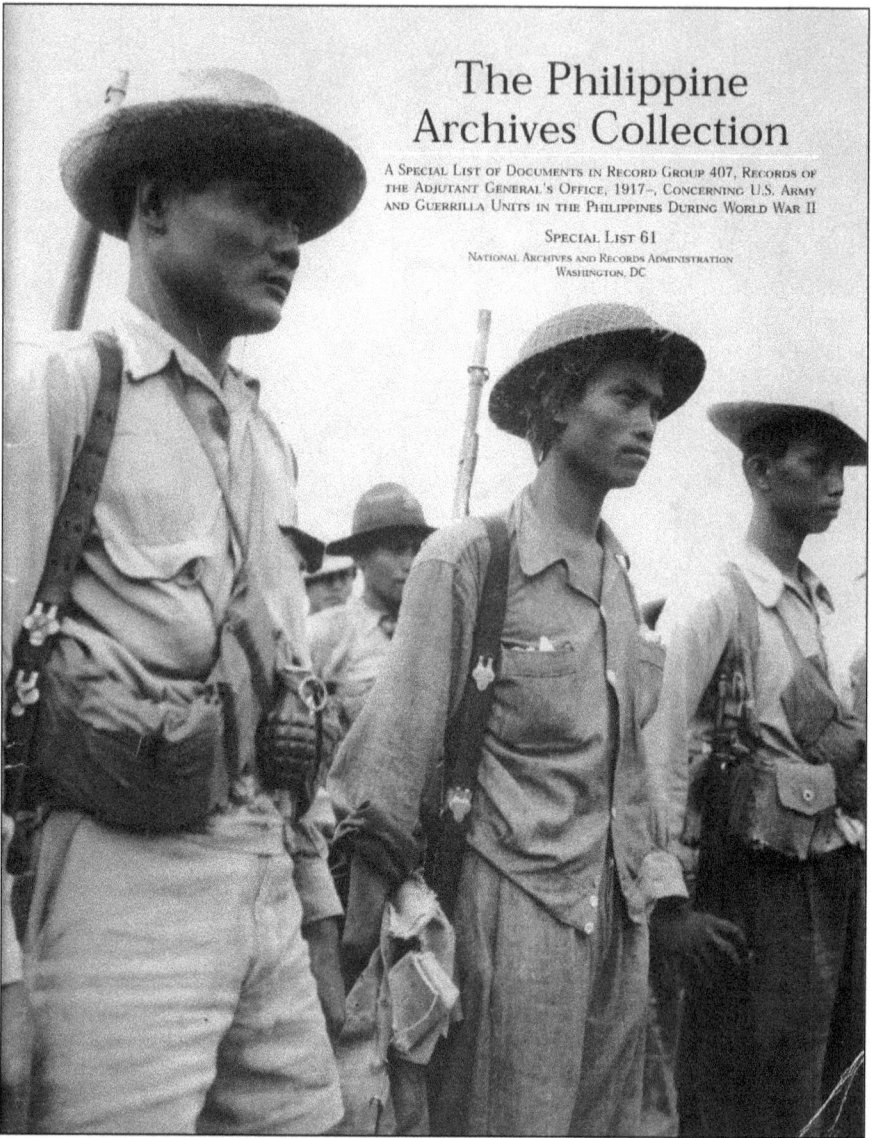

The Philippine
Archives Collection

A SPECIAL LIST OF DOCUMENTS IN RECORD GROUP 407, RECORDS OF
THE ADJUTANT GENERAL'S OFFICE, 1917–, CONCERNING U.S. ARMY
AND GUERRILLA UNITS IN THE PHILIPPINES DURING WORLD WAR II

SPECIAL LIST 61

NATIONAL ARCHIVES AND RECORDS ADMINISTRATION
WASHINGTON, DC

Another group of records of the American government in the Philippines is covered under Record Group 407, "The Philippine Archives Collection." A researcher aid called Special List 61 provides references to several series of documents—some ranging from the 1890s through the 1970s—focusing primarily on Americans and Filipinos who participated in government actions from 1941 (the Japanese invasion) to the end of World War II. Examples of topics in the list include "Military Operations in the Philippines," "Rosters of Guerrillas and Philippine Scouts," "POW Photographs," and "Diaries and Historical Narratives." Many of the records have intrinsic value because of the media used to create the record. For example, due to the shortage of paper from 1941 to 1945, rather than using U.S. War Department forms, the records are on brown paper bags, the backs of other letters, or even on evaporated-milk can labels. This picture, used on the cover of Special List 61, shows Filipino guerrillas who accompanied the 6th Ranger Infantry Battalion on a mission that freed American prisoners from Japanese prison camps on Cabanatuan. Filipinos in America went from being U.S. nationals to U.S. citizen soldiers. (Courtesy of the National Archives and Records Administration.)

Filipinos in the Philippines were taught according to the U.S. educational system. Children were instructed in English, pledged allegiance to the U.S. flag, and memorized significant dates from U.S. history. *Pensionados* and *pensionadas* were the respective names given to a selected group of men and a few women sent to the U.S. for higher education. They were groomed as leaders for the future Philippine nation. While abroad, they received government pensions. Washington, D.C., publications from the 1920s—notably the *Philippine Bulletin* and *Philippine Republic Magazine*—indicate a fierce love of the Philippines and passion for American democracy. Other Filipinos were recruited to staff the emerging 20th century industrial U.S. economy as working class laborers. Filipino men were recruited to join the U.S. Navy in the lowest positions of stewards. (Courtesy of the Cacas family.)

Tomas Rulloda Abellera (1890–1985) was born in the Philippines. He ran away from home at age 17 and joined the U.S. Navy because his parents wanted him to become a priest. In 1916, he married Francisca Estrada (from Astoria, Spain) who was a translator on Wall Street in New York City. Tomas was transferred to Washington, D.C., in 1921, and they lived on Eighth Street, SE, near the Navy Yard. (Courtesy of Evangeline Paredes.)

Fermina Santos came to the United States in 1915 at age five. Her 19-year-old sister Asuncion Santos was working for a Philippine General who was reassigned to Washington, D.C., and asked her to go to the United States with him. She agreed on the condition that she could bring her sister Fermina, pictured here. The sisters began their journey to America (pages 31, 63, and 64). (Courtesy of the Toribio family.)

While Filipino U.S. nationals were prohibited from becoming U.S. citizens, second-generation Filipinos born in the United States in the early 20th century were American citizens by birth. Pictured on the left is Aurora Quezon (page 30), first lady of the Philippine Commonwealth. On the right is Evangeline "Vangie" Abellera, who was born in Brooklyn, New York, in 1916, daughter of Tomas and Francisca Abellera (page 14). Vangie witnessed many of the historic, political, and governmental events that were occurring in Washington, D.C., in the mid-20th century. (Courtesy of Evangeline Paredes.)

Rosa Espina was born in Washington, D.C., in 1924. Her father, Apolonio Espina, was already in America, having joined the U.S. Navy in the early 1900s. At age 14, she married 28-year-old Alfonso "Al" Bautista (1910–1987), who came to the United States in 1927, and they had seven children. When he was not driving a taxicab in Washington, Al, a jazz musician, played the double bass. (Courtesy of the Cacas family.)

Florentine Calabia (1898–1980) seated on the far left, ran away from home at age 16 to join the U.S. Navy in World War I and became a submarine torpedo gunner's mate. He quipped, "Pinoys were so small they fit in the torpedo tubes." Later he became a Coney Island prizefighter (bantam weight) and then moved to Washington, D.C., in the 1930s (pages 30, 35, and 49). He is pictured here with his church group in the mid-1920s. (Courtesy of the Calabia family.)

Crisanto Relucio joined the U.S. Navy in 1919 and served on the USS *Mayflower*, a ship that was commissioned for the Spanish-American War. At the time of his service, the USS *Mayflower* functioned as the presidential yacht for Calvin Coolidge. Crisanto fathered four children in Washington, D.C., and after daughter Doris Eleanor was born (see below), he left the family, remarried, and lived in San Diego, California. (Courtesy of the Toribio family.)

HEALTH DEPARTMENT OF THE DISTRICT OF COLUMBIA

Certificate of Birth Registration

This is to Certify, That in accordance with an Act to provide for the better registration of births in the District of Columbia and for other purposes, approved March 1, 1907, the birth of a   Female child to   Chrisanto & Dorrance Relucio, on Aug. 29, 1926   has been officially registered in the Health Office of the District of Columbia, by   Cyrus R. Creveling, M. D.
        Name of Child   – DORRANCE ELLONORE RELUCIO –
Record No. 296244

Date of filing Aug. 31, 1926   Health Officer.

To

Dorrance Ellonore [sic] Relucio was born on August 29, 1926, at the Casualty Hospital (705 Massachusetts Avenue) in Washington, D.C. The daughter of Crisanto Relucio (pictured at the top of this page) and 20-year-old Doris Peckham of Washington, D.C., she was baptized on October 24th in St. Peter's Church on Capitol Hill. Her parents separated shortly afterwards. Family records show that "Doris Eleonore" was adopted by a Filipino couple, Asuncion and Generoso Gaudiel (page 64), for $500 and renamed Amparing Santos Gaudiel (1926–2001). She studied nursing at Mercy Hospital in Baltimore, Maryland. In 1949, Amparing married Leonilo Toribio (pages 38 and 65), and they raised their family in rural Accokeek, Maryland. Longtime Maryland residents, the extended family (page 111) has since settled on Cobb Island, on the Maryland side of the Potomac River. (Courtesy of the Toribio family.)

Dave Apollon, a Russian musician, sailed to the Philippines in 1911 to start his music career. In the 1920s, he went to New York City and hired a group of talented young Filipino string musicians to accompany his show. Apollon later played with legendary jazz musician Django Reinhardt. Here the Filipino musicians pose for a portrait after a performance at Radio City Music Hall in New York. The original photograph was inscribed to Juanito Paredes (page 60) and the musicians identified on the back of the photograph are Loy Silagon, Carlos Quiambao, Peping Hernandez (page 62), Harold Aloma, Ben del Rosario, Gregory Davidoff, Ponce Espiritu, Manuel Enriquez, Silvestre Ramido, and Francisco Castro. (Courtesy of Evangeline Paredes.)

A group of Filipino Naval Academy athletes gathered after a game of basketball. Mariano Peji (page 19) was active in academy entertainment and athletics and is pictured here (first row, second from the right) with his colleagues, taken around the late 1920s. (Courtesy of the Toribio family.)

The Filipino-American Friendly Association was established in 1928 at the U.S. Naval Academy (USNA) in Annapolis, Maryland. Mariano Peji is in the back row of the photograph above and in the center of the group of three sailors. He came to the United States in the 1920s when he joined the U.S. Navy. Peji served as a steward at the USNA and married Fermina Santos (page 31) in 1924. They owned restaurants and homes in Annapolis, Maryland, and Portsmouth, Virginia. Peji passed away in the mid-1980s. (Courtesy of the Toribio family.)

Alfredo Sabino (1902–1987) joined the U.S. Navy in 1921 and worked as a steward. He is the sailor on the left in the photograph on the left. Alfredo served on the presidential yacht *Sequoia* for Pres. Franklin Roosevelt and was chief steward for two secretaries of the U.S. Navy during the 1930s and 1940s. He retired in 1952 after 29 years and married Rose Kershner. They had three children and settled their family on Dorchester Street in Glassmanor, Maryland. Alfredo's daughter is Sandy Sabino Chinn, and his granddaughter is Lisa Chinn (pages 86, 99, and 114). (Courtesy of Sandra Sabino Chinn.)

Silvestre Braga Brazal (1906–1995) joined the U.S. Navy in 1928 at age 22 and was a steward on the USS *Henderson* and later on the USS *Williamsburg*, Harry Truman's presidential yacht. Shown below is Brazal's Declaration of Intention (Form 2202) used to apply for U.S. citizenship in 1937. Brazal married Helen McGonagle in 1947 and had two daughters, Monica (b. 1948) and Elena (b. 1949) (page 71). The Brazals raised their family in southeast D.C., and daughter Elena continues to live in the family's first home on Kentucky Avenue, SE; Monica lives in the family's second home in Suitland, Maryland. (Courtesy of Monica Brazal Menard.)

| File or Service No. | Surname, First Name and Initial | Class | Design |

PAY AND ALLOWANCES INFORMATION

PERSONAL WITHDRAWAL MEMORANDUM

CREDITS				DUE (OR OVERPAID)		DRAWN	
				DATE	AMOUNT	DATE	AMOU
CCk(PA)(18) 7/27/41	179 40						
S & FSD	27 60						
Avia/SM							
S&FSD (Avia) (S/M)							
OTHER CREDITS:							
Subs @ 1.20	36 00						
Total Credits	$ 243 00						
CHECKAGES							
ALLOTMENTS:							
N-1/43-IND	8 70						
Family Allowances A	22 00						
OTHER CHECKAGES:							
Total Checkages	$ 30 70						
NET PAY PER MONTH	$ 212 30						

Fold IN

DISBURSING OFFICER: This is a *MEMORANDUM ONLY.* Do *NOT SIGN, STAMP, ENDORSE* or *MAKE PAYMENT* on this card. Use *ONLY* as an aid in reconstructing lost pay record but *NOT in lieu* the required sworn statement *NOR* in lieu of the required pay record.

One of the largest areas of employment for Filipinos in the first half of the 20th century was in the U.S. Navy, given the presence of major naval bases along coastal shores of Maryland and Virginia. Filipinos also worked in the U.S. War Department, the precursor to the department of defense. Many Filipinos enlisted in the U.S. Navy while they were still in the Philippines because it gave them greater economic opportunities and a chance to see the world. Given that the dollar was twice the value of the peso, a Filipino steward in the U.S. Navy earned more money than a high-ranking officer in the Philippine armed forces. This is an April 1944 pay slip for seaman Alfredo Sabino (page 20). (Courtesy of Sandra Sabino Chinn.)

Fernando V. Aguilar (1905–1996) came to the United States in 1926 and, with his uncle, became a union leader during the Great Depression. In search of adventure, he went to Yosemite National Park, became a cook at the Ahwanee Hotel, and played tennis with prominent hotel guests. His family settled in the D.C. area in the mid-1930s when Aguilar drove a taxicab. (Photograph by and courtesy of Rita M. Cacas, 1993.)

Patricio Guibao (1909–2007) came to the United States in 1928. He arrived in Washington, D.C., in 1934 and pursued a bachelor of arts degree and a master of arts degree in accounting at Catholic University of America and was a night laborer at the U.S. Bureau of Engraving and Printing. In 1942, he was drafted into the U.S. Army as a record keeper. From 1946 until 1966, Guibao was an accountant and tax auditor for the D.C. government. (Photograph by and courtesy of Rita Cacas, 1993.)

Maximino "Max" Cacho Cacas (1907–1944) came to the United States in 1926; studied accounting at the University of California, Berkeley; and graduated in 1933. Filipinos on the Pacific Coast were restricted from becoming professionals by anti-Filipino laws, so when he applied for accounting jobs, he was told that "Filipinos don't do that kind of work." Max left California for Washington, D.C., with his brother Clemente (page 25) in the late 1930s but was not there for long. As a U.S. Army sergeant, he died in service during World War II in the Pacific theater. (Courtesy of the Cacas family.)

Bibiano Bitanga (1905–2005) arrived in 1927 and worked in a cannery. He went to Chicago and attended Loyola University and the St. Louis Institute—a YWCA organization specializing in services to immigrant and foreign communities housed in the Jane Addams Hull House in Chicago—but could not afford to finish school. He moved to Washington, D.C., in 1935 and worked at the U.S. Bureau of Engraving and Printing. He graduated from the National University School of Law, which became George Washington University Law School. Bitanga never married and lived with the DePeralta family (page 70). (Courtesy of Maria DePeralta Ferrara.)

Clemente Cacas (1910–1995) came to the United States in 1929 at age 19 to join his brother Maximino (page 24) in Berkeley. He worked on farms but sought adventure beyond California. On his journey east, he visited Minnesota and left because "it was too cold for Filipinos." Cacas lived briefly in Chicago and had the souvenir portrait above right taken at the 1933 Chicago World's Fair. His story continues on pages 34 and 72. (Courtesy of the Cacas family.)

Moises Bautista (1909–2000) also came to the United States to be with his brother Alfonso, who arrived in 1927, and his friend Maximino Cacas (page 24). The Cacas and Bautista brothers were childhood friends in Narvacan, Philippines. All four men enlisted in the U.S. Army at the start of World War II. Moises married Monica Selga (page 85) in 1952, and they lived in Suitland, Maryland. (Courtesy of the Cacas family.)

The Tydings-McDuffie Act of 1934 raised the status of the Philippines from a U.S. territory to a commonwealth, with the promise of independence within 10 years. As transition to full independence, the Philippine Commonwealth was established, which was a prerequisite to the Philippine Republic. In elections held on September 15, 1935, Manuel L. Quezon (left) was chosen president and Sergio Osmena vice president of the commonwealth. Inauguration ceremonies were held on November 15, 1935, in front of the legislative building in Manila as Chief Justice Ramon Avanceña (left) administers the Oath of Office to Quezon. A direct path to independence, however, was interrupted and put on hold by World War II. Filipinos in America could not communicate with family and friends in the Philippines during the war years. In 1943 after continuing advocacy to join the U.S. military, Filipinos in America were allowed to enlist in various branches. The Japanese invaded the Philippines in 1941, defeating Gen. Douglas MacArthur at Bataan and Corregidor, and Quezon established a government-in-exile in Washington, D.C., creating a new wave of Filipinos settling in the nation's capital. (Courtesy of the National Archives and Records Administration.)

Mateo Perez (1908–1995) arrived in the United States in 1929. He immediately went to Washington, D.C., and stayed with family friend Camilo Osias (whose father was the Philippine resident commissioner) and attended Central (now Cardozo) High School. Mateo worked as a butler to Rear Admiral Ridley McLean of the U.S. Navy but, after the admiral's death in 1933, worked in the Philippine Resident Commissioner's Office (pictured here) and married Consuelo Laconsay (1912–2004) (page 45). (Courtesy of Mateo Perez.)

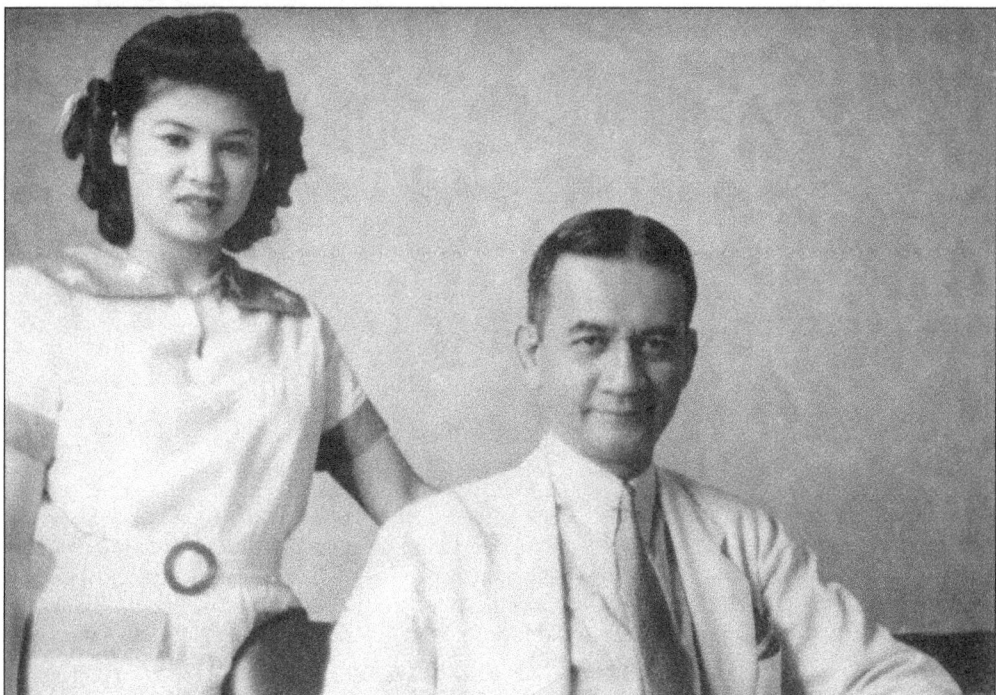

Evangeline "Vangie" Abellera (page 15) attended George Washington University in the mid-1930s and worked as a telephone operator in the Philippine Resident Commissioner's Office, which later became the Philippine Embassy. When World War II began, she was President Quezon's secretary (page 58). Abellera is pictured here with Francisco Varona, an elected representative of the Philippine Legislature from 1931 until 1934. (Courtesy of Evangeline Paredes.)

Reception and Dance in honor of Col. Carlos P. Romulo,
Resident Commissioner of the Philippines to the United States.
Sponsored by The Filipino Executive Council of Washington D.C.
MAYFLOWER HOTEL — SEPT. 23, 1944

The social scene of the 1930s was in full swing, and Filipinos enjoyed comfortable middle-class lives in social Washington, D.C. Extravagant parties were common during the 1930s, and to celebrate the fourth anniversary of the Commonwealth of the Philippines the Filipinos of Washington, D.C., sponsored a dinner and dance for over 400 people at the National Press Club

on November 18, 1939. In this picture, five years later, an even larger community of professionals, the Filipino Executive Council of Washington, D.C., sponsors a dinner and dance in honor of Col. Carlos Romulo (standing, center, first row) at the Mayflower Hotel, September 23, 1944. (Courtesy of the Toribio family.)

The Filipino Women's Club of Washington, D.C., was formed in 1943, and Nestora Calabia (first row, second from the right) was elected president. On October 6, 1943, the board of directors invited the Philippine Commonwealth president's wife, Aurora Quezon (seated, center), to be guest speaker. Also in attendance was Sofia Reyes De Veyra (second row, third from the right), whose husband, Jaime Carlos De Veyra, was the former resident commissioner (1917–1923). In another event hosted by the women's club, Mrs. De Veyra gave an eloquent speech reported in the *Filipino Club Bulletin* in which a Caucasian woman exclaimed, "Why, I had no idea that Filipino women were refined, cultured, or even educated." The *Philippine Republic* magazine reported that the De Veyra children easily transitioned into the American school system because they had been so well groomed and educated in the Philippines. (Courtesy of the Calabia family.)

Florentine Calabia was already living in the United States and returned to the Philippines to marry Nestora Monfero (1912–2004), whose family owned a coconut plantation. They came to Washington, D.C., in the early 1930s. Here they pose for a picture at Union Station in front of the statue of Christopher Columbus (pages 16 and 49). (Courtesy of the Calabia family.)

José Rizal is a revered national hero of the Philippines, having been a strong advocate and leader of reforms during the Spanish colonial era. His 1896 trial and execution made him a martyr of the Philippine Revolution of 1898, and the anniversary of his death is commemorated as a Philippine holiday. Here the Santos sisters (page 14), with their spouses, join friends in observing the holiday on December 30, 1947. At the far left are Gil Esposo with his wife, Asuncion Santos, and the second couple from the right is her sister Fermina with her husband, Mariano Peji (page 19). (Courtesy of the Toribio family.)

Fermina Santos (page 14) operated a boardinghouse and restaurant near the U.S. Naval Academy in Annapolis in the early 1920s. She met and married Mariano Peji (page 19), a U.S. Navy man, in 1924. They opened several restaurants (page 63) and never felt the hardships of the Great Depression. A 1935 Annapolis news clipping documented Fermina as hostess for the Filipino Social Club of Annapolis. (Courtesy of the Toribio family.)

INAUGURAL BALL
THE FILIPINO NATIONALS COUNCIL
HOTEL ASTOR

Filipinos began establishing a solid presence along the East Coast. Pictured here is the inaugural ball of the Filipino Nationals Council of New York, at the Astor Hotel in 1941. Within the next

year, World War II was approaching, and Filipinos answered the call to support their adopted homeland. (Courtesy of the Toribio family.)

At the onset of World War II, the Japanese invaded the Philippines on December 8, 1941. Filipino nationals living in America signed up to fight alongside American soldiers for the protection of their homeland. Here, Clemente Cacas (page 25), right, enlisted in the U.S. Army in 1941 in New York City, where he lived. A member of the Filipino Nationals Council of New York (pages 32 and 33), Cacas was drafted and served at a military hospital in Van Nuys, California. He incurred a medical disability for which he received an honorable discharge in 1945, and became eligible for citizenship. His certificate of naturalization is shown below. After his military service, Cacas moved back to Washington, D.C., and lived on Capitol Hill, where he became a taxicab driver and married Maria Bello (pages 34, 47, and 71). (Courtesy of the Cacas family.)

Two

FILIPINOS IN THE
WASHINGTON, D.C.,
WORKFORCE

Early Filipinos arrived and settled in the Washington, D.C., area between 1900 and 1964. A few came to obtain an education, particularly *pensionados* (page 13) groomed to be future leaders of the Philippines. Most sought paid employment. Filipinos in Washington, D.C., were primarily limited to three areas of work: military service; work in the office of the Philippine resident commissioner; or manual labor and service jobs. In the photograph above, journeymen printers carefully conduct their work at the U.S. Bureau of Engraving and Printing in Washington, D.C. Florentine Calabia, pictured at the end of the left row of workers, looking at the camera, served in the U.S. Navy in World War I (page 16). (Courtesy of the Calabia family.)

Eleanor Roosevelt was a special guest at a December 4, 1943, reception hosted by the Filipino Women's Club of Washington, D.C., to honor Filipinos serving in the U.S. armed forces. U.S. Army fighter pilot Maj. Jesus A. Villamor was recognized for his heroic actions during World War II when he flew one of six fighter planes in an aerial battle over Manila and Batangas, covering General MacArthur and delaying the Japanese attack of the Philippines 12 hours after the bombing of Pearl Harbor on December 7, 1941. Colonel Villamor was one of the pilots who successfully shot down two enemy fighters and one bomber. Shown here at the reception, from left to right, are Nestora Calabia (president of the Filipino Women's Club, page 30), Major Villamor, Eleanor Roosevelt, Aurura Quezon (page 30), and her daughter Maria Aurora "Baby" Quezon. (Courtesy of the Calabia family.)

The Battle of Leyte was a significant amphibious operation of American and Allied forces led by Gen. Douglas MacArthur during World War II. After the Japanese capture of Corregidor in Manila Bay on May 6, 1942, MacArthur vowed to protect the Philippines from further invasion, proclaiming, "I shall return." Two and a half years later, he did. In the historic photograph above, MacArthur and his troops arrived in Leyte, Philippines, on October 20, 1944. The soldier on the right (front) wearing a helmet is M. Sgt. Francisco Salveron (1910–1989), who became a personal aide to Gen. MacArthur. The soldier behind Salveron, also wearing a helmet, is Brig. Gen. Carlos Romulo (pages 67 and 75). After the war, Salveron enlisted in the U.S. Air Force and was assigned to the flight crew of Gen. Dwight D. Eisenhower. He later served as steward to Pres. Harry Truman, as well as to a number of secretaries of defense and state. He settled his family in Bladensburg, Maryland, and retired in 1963; his military honors included a Bronze Star, a Purple Heart, and three Presidential Distinguished Citations. Salveron founded the Gen. Douglas MacArthur post of the Veterans of Foreign Wars of the United States and was its commander for 21 years. This post and the Vicente Lim Post 5471 eventually merged in the late 1980s (pages 75 and 104). Salveron and his wife, Anastasia, are pictured on the right attending the reception honoring the late Philippine president Magsaysay. The reception was sponsored by the Filipino American Fraternity at the Statler Hilton Hotel in 1965 (page 2). (Courtesy of Pedro Sarmiento and the Cacas family.)

Leonilo "Leo" Toribio was born in 1925 in Manila. He joined the U.S. Navy in 1940 and served in World War II. Leo married Amparing Gaudiel (page 17) in 1949. Here they pose for a picture in Mount Vernon, in Alexandria, Virginia, taken shortly after they were married. They had five children and settled in Accokeek, a rural Maryland suburb (pages 65 and 111). (Courtesy of the Toribio family.)

Fidel Gado Herrin (1907–2002) came to the United States in 1927. He enlisted in the U.S. Navy and served in World War II. Herrin came to D.C. in 1947 and was a cook at Walter Reed Army Medical Center, and his wife, pioneer Georgena (1908–2002), was a U.S. Army nurse. They lived in Hyattsville, Maryland. He was a member of the VFW Vicente Lim Post 5471 (page 75). (Photograph by and courtesy of Rita Cacas, 1993.)

Luis Buena (1906–1964) was born in Abra, Philippines. He enlisted in the U.S. Navy in the late 1930s and served in World War II. He married Teresa Mendez in 1948, and they had three daughters. The family settled on Maury Avenue in Oxon Hill, Maryland. Here he poses for a picture in his officer's uniform on F Street in downtown Washington, D.C., in 1948 (pages 53 and 87). (Courtesy of the Buena family.)

Melchor Quidangen (1909–1986) enlisted in the U.S. Navy in the 1930s. He married Felixberta Amigable (1912–1979) before World War II. Melchor became chief steward for Adm. Glenn Davies at the Naval Gun Factory, later called the Naval Weapons Plant, in Anacostia. They lived in the Bellevue (Military) Housing Project on Bolling Air Force Base from 1946 until 1950, then bought a house on Chesapeake Street (page 76) in Washington, D.C., when he retired from the U.S. Navy. Shown here are Mr. and Mrs. Sesinando Guadamor who were also residents of Bellevue. (Courtesy of Clavelina Quidangen Sarmiento.)

Pedro Sarmiento (1906–1998), born in Nueva Ecija, Philippines, joined the U.S. Army (Philippine Scouts Division) in 1935 working on topographic mapping of the Philippines. During World War II, he fought in the Battle of Bataan and survived the death march as a prisoner of war, receiving a Bronze Medal and Purple Heart. He married Cresenciana Calvelo (1908–1979) in 1931. Pictured above in a 1950s family portrait taken in Germany, the couple had eight children and were stationed in the United States and abroad. Their plan was to complete his career with the U.S. Army, then return to the Philippines. When he retired in 1957, however, Cresenciana wanted an American education for their children and to be with the older children who were already living in D.C. They initially settled in Chevy Chase, Maryland. (Left photograph by Rita Cacas, 1993; courtesy of the Sarmiento family.)

Pedro Sarmiento (b. 1933) was born in Manila, Philippines. He joined the U.S. Air Force in 1953 and was a physical science (metallurgy) technician. In 1957, he attended American University on the GI Bill and worked at the National Bureau of Standards (NBS), now the National Institute of Standards and Technology. In 1960, Sarmiento married Clavelina Quidangen (page 77), a Filipina living in D.C. In 1961, a former NBS colleague invited Sarmiento to form a metallurgical lab at the National Aeronautic and Space Administration's Goddard Space Flight Center (Greenbelt, Maryland). He completed his bachelor of arts degree in history and bachelor of science degree in chemistry at the University of Maryland in 1962. Sarmiento was a spectroscopist at Goddard for 21 years and then worked for Bendix Corporation. In 1990, Pedro returned to the federal government as a research chemist for the U.S. Bureau of Engraving and Printing until his retirement in 1997 (page 56). (Courtesy of the Sarmiento family.)

From 1907 until 1946, the Philippine resident commissioner (a position similar to that of Puerto Rico) represented the interests of the Filipinos living in the Philippines and the United States. The commissioner attended sessions of the U.S. Congress in Washington, D.C., but had no voting or veto authority. When World War II began, President Quezon established a Philippine government-in-exile consisting of Filipinos who worked in the office of the Philippine resident commissioner in Washington, D.C., located on Massachusetts Avenue, NW. The Philippines was granted independence from the United States in 1946, and the Philippine Resident Commissioner's Office was formally changed to the Philippine Embassy. This photograph shows the resident commissioner's staff in the late 1930s; Vangie Paredes (page 27) is in the center back row, below the wall lamp. (Courtesy of Evangeline Paredes.)

Philippine president Manuel Quezon (page 26), center, suffered from tuberculosis and went to Saranac Lake, New York, for treatments. Pictured here with President Quezon are close friends, colleagues, and family—his wife, Aurora (page 30), son, Manuel Quezon Jr. (page 81), and daughters Maria Aurora and Maria Zeneida. He died in Saranac Lake on August 1, 1944. He was initially buried in Arlington National Cemetery but was later reinterred in Manila. (Courtesy of Evangeline Paredes.)

A group of well-wishers visit Quezon's successor, Pres. Elpidio Quirino, at Johns Hopkins Hospital in Baltimore, where he was receiving treatments for kidney ailments in the early 1950s. Pioneer Max Corpus—father of Flora Corpuz Nivera (pages 52 and 79)—is at the far left. (Courtesy of Flora Nivera Corpuz.)

Remegio Aqui (1911–1996) was born in Pangasinan, Philippines, and arrived in Washington, D.C., in 1928. After serving in World War II, he became a personal chauffeur to Andrew Mellon, U.S. treasurer, and one of the founders of the National Gallery of Art. He was a former commander of the VFW Vicente Lim Post 5471. He and his wife, Cristeta, settled their family in Hyattsville, Maryland. (Photograph by and courtesy of Rita Cacas, 1993.)

Cesario Savellano (1911–1996) came to Washington in 1928. He was drafted into the U.S. Army and served from 1942 until 1946. After the war, he worked as a cook for Helen Wilson, daughter and heir of Samuel Woodward—a founder of the Woodward and Lothrop department stores. Savellano later worked as a medical records clerk at the National Institutes of Health in Bethesda, Maryland. Savellano lived with the DePeralta family (page 82). (Photograph by and courtesy of Rita Cacas, 1993.)

Mateo Perez (page 27) was living in Washington, D.C., since 1929. He met a relative of the Osias family, Consuelo Laconsay, and they were married in 1931. He retired as a consular's assistant in 1974 after 30 years of service to the Philippine government. This photograph was published in the *Washington Post* accompanying an article by Washington, D.C., chronicler Sarah Booth Conroy on July 25, 1994. (Photograph by and courtesy of Rita Cacas, 1993.)

Leon Alcoy (1918–2002) came to the United States in 1929. He moved to Washington, D.C., in 1931, and was a cook for former U.S. senator Raymond Wells of Missouri. He tried to enlist in World War II but was rejected, as he did not meet minimum weight requirements. He continued to cook and, at night, drove a taxicab. (page 47). (Photograph by and courtesy of Rita Cacas, 1993.)

After serving in the U.S. Army, Moises Bautista joined the National Gallery of Art's guard force in the late 1940s. The 1971 group portrait above shows the guard force on the steps of the West Building mall entrance, February 1954; Moises is fifth from the right in the second row. Bautista retired in 1975. Rita Cacas recalls visiting "uncle" Moises at the gallery as a young adult, wondering what it would be like to work there one day. After completing her bachelor of arts degree in art history, she worked at the gallery from 1979 to 1999. The portrait below was taken when he went back to visit on Veteran's Day, 1994, 20 years after he had retired. He died on June 27, 2000—short of his 91st birthday. (Above photograph, courtesy of the National Gallery of Art, Washington; below photograph, by and courtesy of Rita Cacas.)

It was not uncommon for Filipinos in Washington, D.C., to drive taxicabs after their World War II military service. When he was not working as a security officer at the National Gallery of Art, Moises Bautista (page 46) drove a taxicab. He is pictured in front of his Veterans cab with Clemente Cacas (page 25). After serving in the U.S. Army, they moved to Washington, D.C., bought their own cabs, and drove taxis in the city. Other Filipino cab drivers during this time were Leon Alcoy (page 45), Januario Sevilla (page 50), and Felipe Estifano Mondoñedo. Felipe's daughter Nita Mondoñedo Smith captured endearing stories about the Filipino community during the mid-20th century in two books: *Forever in our Hearts* and *Say Uncle: Life in D.C. with my Filipino Uncles*. The group portrait below was taken at the Filipino Cab Driver's Benefit Dance, at the Willard Hotel in Washington, D.C., on January 22, 1944. Bautista and Cacas were members of the organization while on active duty in World War II. (Above photograph, courtesy of the Cacas family; below photograph, courtesy of the Toribio family.)

Above, the Filipino Capitols and fans pose for a team picture. In an accompanying letter dated August 21, 1947, the team's representative, Francisco Solis, thanks his counterpart, Francisco Alayu, for hosting an athletic meet held in 1947 in Chicago, where they display several of their team's trophies. Solis was born in Pangasinan, Philippines. He lived in Hyattsville, Maryland in the 1940s, and was widely known for organizing some of the largest social events held in Washington, D.C., ballrooms. With the Filipino Capitols, he traveled around the country to play in national tournaments. Two team members pose in the 1945 photograph on the left. Vangie Paredes (page 27) recalled taking the train to Chicago with the baseball team and other D.C. friends. (Above photograph, courtesy of Fran Alayu Womack, Chicago; left photograph, courtesy of Fran Alayu Womack.)

In this early 1940s portrait of the Calabia family, Florentine and Nestora (page 27) pose with their young sons, Florentine "Tino" and Mendell (standing, to the left of his mother). Tino continues his parents' pioneering efforts in Washington, D.C., and New York. He was one of the first Filipino Americans to join the Peace Corps and was a special assistant in the first cabinet of New York mayor John Lindsay in 1966. Tino directed the first national study on *Asian Americans at the U.S. Commission on Civil Rights* in 1976 and served on the board of Pacifica Radio, WPFW (pages 54 and 58). Mendell is a professional photographer in New York City. (Courtesy of the Calabia family.)

Januario Sevilla (1910–1999) came to the United States in 1929 upon joining the U.S. Navy. During World War II he served on Pres. Harry Truman's yacht, the USS *Williamsburg*. A widower, Sevilla married Leona Puyot (widow of D.C. pioneer Lucelo Puyot). He retired after 31 years, worked for the secretary of the Pentagon, drove a D.C. taxi for 40 years, and was a barber for 16 years. Leona was the cousin of Ana Alcoy, page 79. (Photograph by and courtesy of Rita Cacas, 1993.)

Daniel Manantan (1909–1975) was born in La Union, Philippines. He came to the United States in the early 1940s and served in World War II. After the war, he owned a second-floor barbershop (with fellow Filipino, Benny Fontanilla) in Chinatown on Sixth and H Streets. Daniel (front) and his wife, Virginia (seated, left), were the godparents of Samuel (page 101), held by his parents, Maria and Clemente Cacas (page 72) in 1955. (Courtesy of the Cacas family.)

Clavelina "Lee" Quidangen (b. 1934), born in Cavite, Philippines, came to D.C. in 1947. She attended George Washington University and studied home economics, graduating in 1953. Quidangen taught high school in Prince George's County for 30 years. She married Pedro Sarmiento (page 41) in 1960. Here she and her mother, Felixberta (page 76)—a nurse at the George Washington Hospital—visited Mount Vernon in 1948. (Courtesy of Clavelina Sarmiento.)

Consuelo Laconsay (1912–2004) was born in Baguio, Philippines. She came to the United States in 1930 accompanied by an aunt who had already been living in the United States. She married Mateo Perez (page 45) in 1931. Consuelo volunteered with the American Red Cross during World War II, and was a member of the Filipino Women's Club of Washington, D.C. On page 30, she is standing, third from the left. (Photograph by and courtesy of Rita Cacas, 1993.)

Flora Corpuz (b. 1932) was born in the Philippines and came to Washington, D.C., in 1952 to live with her father, Max Corpuz (page 43). Corpuz studied nursing part time for three years at the Catholic University of America and worked at the Emergency Hospital at Seventeenth Street and Massachusetts Avenue near the White House. She recalled that there were only two Filipina nurses there—herself and Revelina Romero. In 1956, Corpuz married Jacinto "Jack" Nivera (1925–2005) who was a White House steward for five U.S. presidents (Eisenhower to Carter). In the photograph below, Nivera poses for a holiday portrait with Rosalyn and Jimmy Carter, taken in the late 1970s. Corpuz recalled that, as family members of the White House staff, they attended picnics and parties on the south lawn of the White House on many occasions. (Courtesy of Flora Corpuz Nivera.)

To Jacinto Nivera,
Best wishes
Rosalynn Carter
Jimmy Carter

Teresa Mendez (1918–1995) was born in Abra, Philippines, and came to Washington, D.C., in 1947 on a nursing fellowship. She married Luis Buena (page 39) in 1948 and settled in Glassmanor, Maryland (page 87). Mendez was a nursing director for geriatric patients at the D.C. Village Hospital in southeast Washington, D.C. (Courtesy of the Buena family.)

Juliana Ordona Panganiban (1912–2000) came to the United States in 1941. She worked as a nanny for American serviceman Lt. Charlie Morton's family from 1941 until 1950. Panganiban lived near St. Mary's Church on Fourth Street. She married D.C. pioneer Rudy Panganiban in 1944, and bought the stone house next to the Riversdale Mansion in Riverdale, Maryland, that may have been the mansion caretaker's residence. (Photograph by and courtesy of Rita Cacas, 1993.)

Nestora Monfero taught school in the Philippines before she married Florentine Calabia. She studied law at Southeastern University in D.C., graduated in 1937, and became an auditor at the General Accounting Office—the predecessor agency to the Government Accountability Office. After working more than 30 years, she was passed up for promotions and initiated a class-action suit against the government that resulted in a very large settlement in the 1970s (pages 16, 30, and 49). (Courtesy of the Calabia family.)

Alex DePeralta (b. 1915) came to Washington, D.C., in 1949 and served in the U.S. Army, in World War II and the Korean War. He was stationed in France (1950s) and moved his family there for two years. After his service, he used the GI bill to attend Southeastern University, where he studied commerce and business administration (1960–1962). He worked for the U.S. Department of Interior and retired in 1972 (page 82). (Courtesy of the Cacas family.)

The federal government was a major employer during the early 20th century, particularly with the creation of new programs and agencies from the New Deal. A basic requirement for federal employment was and still is U.S. citizenship. U.S.-born whites and blacks were automatically citizens. White immigrants could become U.S. citizens. Black immigration was almost nonexistent. Before 1943, first-generation Filipinos in America were neither citizens nor immigrants eligible to become citizens. Filipinos who had enlisted in military service prior to this period were eligible for federal employment when they left or completed their service. Pictured above, a dinner and dance was given in honor of Philippine and U.S. government employees on November 22, 1952, held at the Wardman Park Hotel in Washington, D.C. (Courtesy of Maria DePeralta Ferrara.)

Bibiano Bitanga became eligible for federal employment in 1928 but said, "The wages were low: 10¢ per hour." In 1930, he was a file clerk at the newly established Department of Veterans Affairs in Washington, D.C., but he said, "This was not a position; it was just a job." In 1934, he was furloughed to the U.S. Bureau of Engraving and Printing while attending law school (page 24). (Photograph by and courtesy of Rita Cacas, 1993.)

Filipinos made valuable contributions in the public and private sectors during the transition from President Kennedy's New Frontier and President Johnson's Great Society. Pedro Sarmiento (page 56) was well respected for his work in spectroscopy at NASA's Goddard Space Flight Center in Greenbelt, Maryland. In 1967, he devised a new way to conduct diffraction studies that led to the development of a specialized Polaroid reflection camera. The use of this new type of camera reduced critical time needed during photography and X-ray processing, saving the government over $4,000 at that time. Since his retirement in 1997, Sarmiento has been a professional docent at the Smithsonian Institution's National Air and Space Museum in D.C. (Photograph by Rita Cacas, 2009; courtesy of the Sarmiento family.)

Passage of Title VII of the Civil Rights Act of 1964 meant federal equal employment opportunity policies and programs, leading to the recruitment of minorities and women into federal positions between 1965 and 1971. Here Crisanto Basilio (b. 1926) receives an award in 1981 from U.S. Department of Housing and Urban Development Secretary Moon Landrieu. He was hired in 1971 as a clerk in the executive secretariat's office, and served six U.S. Department of Housing and Urban Development secretaries until his retirement in 1988 (page 68). (Courtesy of Crisanto Basilio.)

Maria Bello (b. 1929) married Clemente Cacas and came to D.C. in 1954 (page 72). A homemaker and seamstress, she and Clemente raised four children on a taxicab driver's salary, and sent them to Catholic school. In 1971, Maria was recruited into a clerical position at the U.S. Department of Housing and Urban Development. Here she receives an Employee of the Month award in 1981 from Marie Kissick, the administration director. Maria retired from the U.S. Department of Housing and Urban Development in 1992. (Courtesy of Maria Cacas.)

Florentine "Tino" Calabia (b. 1935, Washington, D.C.), son of Florentine and Nestora Calabia (pages 30 and 49), attended St. Martin's Catholic School, receiving scholarships to Gonzaga College High School and Georgetown University. Tino has worked for the U.S. Department of Housing and Urban Development (HUD) as a federal agency coordinator since 1995. His godfather was Quentin Paredes, Philippine resident commissioner in 1935, who was related to the husband of Vangie Paredes, Juanito Paredes (page 60). Vangie, right, was as an executive secretary in the Philippine Resident Commissioner's Office in the mid-1930s. After Philippine independence was declared in 1946, the office became the Philippine Embassy, and Vangie was the public relations officer. When she wanted to retire from the Philippine government (1936–1957), Vangie was offered full benefits under the conditions of giving up U.S. citizenship. She chose not to and worked for the Pentagon for more than 30 years as a secretary. Upon her retirement in 1991, Vangie received the highest civilian award given by the secretary of defense. (Photograph by Christopher Cook, 2009.)

Three

ESTABLISHING D.C.
FILIPINO COMMUNITIES

This chapter depicts the increased migration and visibility of Filipino women who joined Filipino men to start families, especially after World War II. These pioneers raised their families, playing key roles in establishing permanent communities and becoming part of the civic life of the larger Washington, D.C., community into the 1960s and 1970s. They married in Catholic churches, baptized their U.S.-born children, and sent them to parochial schools. These parents joined social clubs that included sewing circles, choirs, baseball teams, dance troupes, and veteran organizations. Above, four Filipina war brides who arrived between 1947 and 1954 attend a social event during the 1960s: unidentified, Maria Cacas (page 72), Monica Bautista (page 85), Florentina dePeralta (page 82), and Ana Alcoy (page 79). (Courtesy of the Cacas family.)

During World War II, Philippine president Manuel Quezon established the Philippine government-in-exile in 1941 in Washington, D.C. Vangie Abellera (page 27) and Juanito Paredes worked there. They married in 1941 and are shown in the portrait on the left, taken at their home on Chesapeake Street, SE. Paredes was the nephew of Quentin B. Paredes (1884–1973), who was the Philippine resident commissioner to Washington, D.C., in 1935. Abellera's father, Thomas Abellera (page 14) owned a house on Forrester St., SE. In the group photograph above, government-in-exile staff gather after work in front of the house. At the far left is Urbano Zafra, who was Quezon's economic advisor, and his wife. Vangie is in the center; to her left is Benigno Aquino Sr., who was the father-in-law of Pres. Corazon Aquino (11th Philippine president from 1986 until 1992), who was renting Thomas's house at that time. (Courtesy of Evangeline Paredes.)

The *Washington Star* reported on September 18, 1949, that "the Philippine Ambassador, Mr. J. M. Elizalde escorted Miss Dolores Lillian Abellera when she became the bride of Mr. Nolasco Icarangal. The wedding took place at St. Matthew's Cathedral. The couple have [sic] been connected with the Philippine government since 1937." Joaquín Elizalde (1896–1965), pictured above in the center, was appointed Philippine resident commissioner to fill the vacancy caused by the resignation of Quintin Paredes in 1938, serving until 1944. The bride, Dolores Abellera (to the right of Elizalde), is Vangie Paredes's sister; Paredes is the bridesmaid at the far right. The photograph below shows the lavish party held at the embassy. Paredes recalled that Elizalde had all the women's dresses custom made for the event. Abellera is on the far right dancing with her new husband, Icarangal (kneeling). (Courtesy of Evangeline Paredes.)

Filipinos were performers in D.C. bands and orchestras. Peping Hernandez sent this photograph to his cousin Leo Toribio (page 38), a U.S. Navy sailor stationed in Patuxent River, Maryland in 1949. Hernandez was also a member of Dave Apollon's Filipino Orchestra, and is identified in the portrait at Radio City Music Hall (on the back of the photograph, page 18) as the third musician from the left. (Courtesy of the Toribio family.)

Clavelina "Lee" Quidangen (pages 51 and 77) attended Kramer Junior High School and Anacostia High School (both located in southeast D.C.), where she graduated in 1958. In this picture, Quidangen—at the end of the fourth row, first on the left—is shown with other members of the Kramer High School Glee Club in 1950. (Courtesy of Clavelina Sarmiento.)

Longtime restaurateurs Mariano and Fermina Peji (page 31) are shown here at their Light House Café and Manila House in Portsmouth, Virginia, during the 1940s. They also owned restaurants in Annapolis where they first met and in New York during the 1930s. Their niece Amparing (page 17) attended the Woodrow Wilson High School in Portsmouth, worked at the restaurant at the time, and is shown above (at the far left) with a school friend. The café menu shows variations of home cooked Filipino (Polynesian), Chinese, and American food at post-Depression prices. (Courtesy of the Toribio family.)

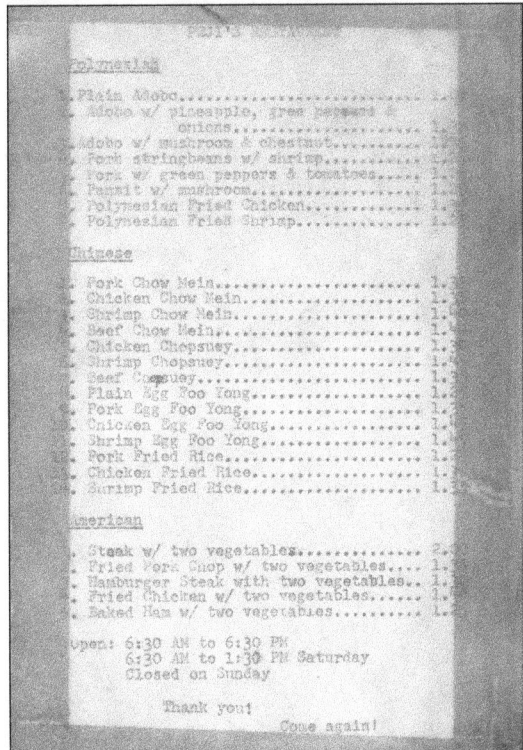

Asuncion "Manang" Gaudiel (page 14), born around the late 1890s and considered the pioneer of the Toribio family (page 111), came to the United States in 1915. She married Generoso Gaudiel in the 1930s, and they were childless. When Doris Relucio was born to young parents, it was Manang who adopted her, raising her as Amparing Gaudiel (page 17). After her marriage to Gaudiel ended, she married Gil Esposo. They opened the Manila House in downtown D.C., where she became affectionately known as *Manang*, which means older sister in the Ilocano language. The Manila House became a haven for bachelors to eat home-cooked meals and enjoy the company of fellow Filipinos. In the late-1940s group photograph below, Manang is second from the left at the shared dining table of the Manila House. She passed away in 1960. (Courtesy of the Toribio family.)

Young Filipino families' dreams included owning their own home with access to public transportation and good schools. Above, newlyweds Leo and Amparing Toribio (page 38) read issues of *Baby Talk* magazine, and await the birth of their first child. They bought their first home at 903 G Street, SE, in the late 1940s, after Leo completed his service with the U.S. Navy. Amparing graduated from Mercy Hospital in Baltimore and began working as a nurse at the old Providence Hospital. Leonila, or Nila, was born in 1950, and she is pictured in the photograph at right with her father on the front porch of their new home. Nila is also pictured at a White House event on page 124. (Courtesy of the Toribio family.)

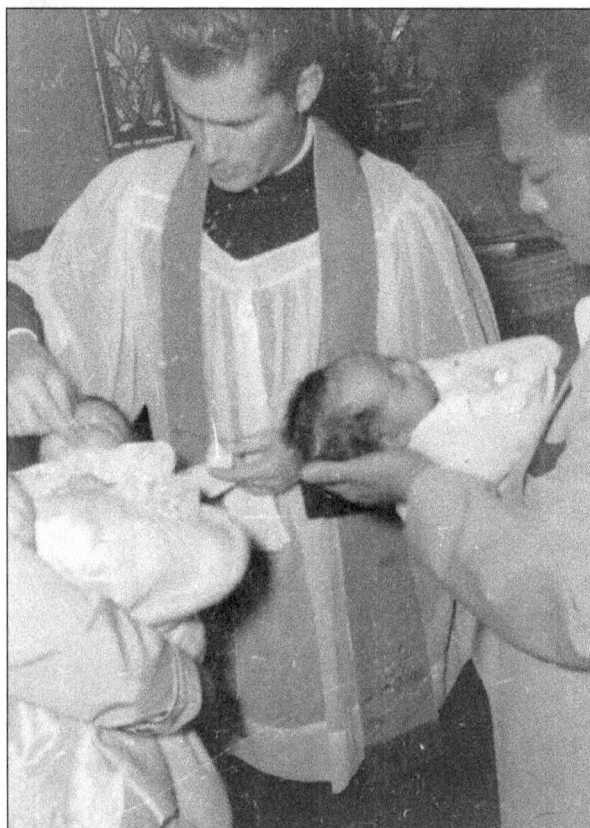

Cousins Leonila "Nila" Toribio and Christina Berg were baptized at St. Peter's Catholic Church on Capitol Hill in 1950—the same church where Nila's mother, Amparing (back row, left), was baptized in 1926 (page 17). In the photograph above, baby Nila is on the left, held by her godfather, Gil Roxas, and with her two godmothers, Marie DeLa Cruz and Mary Cook. Godparents Mariano and Fermina Peji (page 31) hold Christina. Also in the back row are Nila's father, Leo, and her grandmother Manang, who owned the Manila House restaurant (page 64). (Courtesy of the Toribio family.)

The Filipino Women's Club of Washington D.C. (page 30) hosted a luncheon in honor of the Foreign University Women Delegates to the Triennial Conference of the International Federation of University Women on August 9, 1947, at the Willard Hotel's Congressional Room. The arrangements committee included club president Nestora Calabia (page 54), sixth from the left, and Vangie Paredes (page 15), second from the right. (Courtesy of the Calabia family.)

Gen. Carlos Romulo, Philippine secretary of foreign affairs and president of the United Nations General Assembly, received the Cardinal Gibbons Medal in 1950 from Rev. Patrick O'Boyle, Archbishop of Washington, D.C. The medal is awarded for distinguished service to the Catholic Church, the United States, or Catholic University. Pictured are Romulo's sons Roberto and Ricardo, Mrs. Romulo, General Romulo, Archbishop O'Boyle, and son Gregorio Romulo (pages 29 and 75). (Courtesy of the National Archives and Records Administration.)

Friends and family celebrate the christening of Max Cacas (b. 1954; also pictured on page 78) with his parents, Maria and Clemente (back row, right) at their apartment on Minnesota Avenue, SE. Pictured here are D.C. pioneers Juliana Panganiban, Nena DePeralta; Cristeta and Remegio Aqui; Osmundo and Maria Cabigas; Ana Alcoy; Monica Bautista; Pete Augustin; and Joe and Leona Puyot. (Courtesy of the Cacas family.)

Women got together for an afternoon of sewing projects. At the left (white blouse) is Manang (page 64); Leona Sevilla, seventh from the left; Juliana Panganiban, ninth from the left (page 51); and Consuelo Perez, tenth from the right (page 49). Sitting, first on the right is Mrs. Jaime Hernandez, whose husband was financial advisor to General Romulo (page 67). Many of the women pictured here were also members of the Filipino Women's Club of Washington (page 30). (Courtesy of the Calabia family.)

Unidentified newlyweds posed for this family portrait in the 1940s. While many Filipinos came to Washington, D.C., others first settled on the West Coast, the Midwest (Chicago), the South (New Orleans), or East Coast (New York). Those with the U.S. armed forces sometimes came from assignments in other nations. Like other pioneer Filipino communities in the nation that were mainly single males who married non-Filipino women, the pioneer community in the Washington, D.C., area was interracial. On the other hand, there were notable marriages in Washington, D.C., between Filipino women and non-Filipino men, including Loida Nicholas and Reginald Lewis (author and chairman/CEO of TLC Beatrice International) as well as Cecilia Suyat and Thurgood Marshall (lead attorney for the historic 1954 *Brown v. Board of Education* Supreme Court decision and the first African American U.S. Supreme Court Justice in 1967. (Courtesy of the Toribio family.)

Cornelio Lopez (1904–1995), left, arrived to the United States in the early 1920s and graduated from the University of Iowa Law School in 1927. In the early 1960s, Cornelio's son Manuel could not legally marry a white woman due to Maryland antimiscegenation laws. So he fought to repeal the laws. Cornelio is pictured here attending a New Year's Eve party with Alex and Florentina DePeralta (page 82), and Cesario Savellano (page 44) sitting to the right. (Courtesy of Maria DePeralta Ferrara.)

FILIPINO EXECUTIVE COUNCIL COMMONWEALTH DANCE. NATIONAL PRESS AUDITORIUM. WASHINGTON, D.C. NOV. 15 1944
DIOSDADO M YAP, PRESIDENT.   BERNARD DE GUIA, COMMITTEE CHAIRMAN

In several panoramic photographs taken at parties attended by hundreds of people, it is interesting to note that white women were often with Filipino men, but white men were not photographed with Filipino women during the 1940s and 1950s. This may have been due to the late arrival of Filipino women to the United States until after World War II. The above photograph is from a detail of the Filipino Executive Council at a dinner and dance held at the National Press Club in Washington, D.C., on November 15, 1944. (Courtesy of the Toribio family.)

Crisanto Basilio (b. 1926) joined the U.S. Navy in 1945 and was stationed at the Naval Barracks in Annapolis. He and Carol Diven were married in Rhode Island in 1950. After serving in the U.S. Navy for 22 years, he retired in 1966 and settled his family in Oxon Hill, Maryland, in 1970 to work at the U.S. Department of Housing and Urban Development (page 55). (Courtesy of Crisanto Basilio.)

Silvestre Brazal (page 21) married Helen McGonagle in 1947 in Elkton, Maryland. Pictured with daughters Elena (above left) and Monica in 1953, they enjoy a formal invitation from President Truman to cruise on his presidential yacht, the USS *Williamsburg*—the same ship on which Brazal served as a steward. Helen was a founding member of the VFW Post 5471 Ladies Auxiliary (page 104); Monica, pictured above sitting on her mother's lap and pictured recently on the right, followed her mother's footsteps and is currently the three-term president of the Ladies Auxiliary. (Above photograph, courtesy of Monica Brazal Menard; below photograph, by and courtesy of Rita Cacas, 2009.)

Cacas Bello Wedding
Jan. 18 1954
With Families, Relatives, Sponsors, Maids & Friends
Santa, Ilocos Sur.

Between 1929 and the early 1950s, Clemente Cacas (1910–1995; also pictured on page 25) lived all over the United States, including San Francisco, Minnesota, Chicago, and New York; served in the U.S. Army in World War II; enjoyed a bachelor's life; and worked in Washington, D.C., as a taxicab driver. At age 43, Clemente's cousin in the Philippines wanted him to settle down, so she arranged a marriage for him to one of their neighbors. When Clemente went back home, however, he attended another party, met and fell in love with Maria Bello, 19 years his junior, and asked her to marry him instead. Here family and town mates from Santa Ilocus Sur gather for a wedding portrait on January 18, 1954. The couple settled in Glassmanor, Maryland, where they raised four children (pages 78 and 86). (Courtesy of the Cacas family.)

Mr. Eugenio Cacas
request the honor of your presence
at the marriage of his
son
Clemente
to
Miss Maria Bello

Mr. & Mrs. Manuel Bello
request the honor of your presence
at the marriage of their
daughter
Maria
to
Mr. Clemente Cacas

to be solemnized at the Catholic Church of Santa, Ilocos Sur, on Monday morning
the 18 of January, 1954, at 6:00 o'clock, and the wedding
reception to be held at the Bride's residence

The least expensive method of transportation from the Philippines to the United States was by ocean liner that took over twenty days. Newlyweds Clemente and Maria Cacas (page 72) traveled to the United States via the USS *President Wilson*; shown here is her ticket for the trip. Already pregnant with their first child, they traveled with Maria's aunt, Puresa, and Puresa's baby, Janet, is shown here on Maria's lap. In her daily journal that began on June 18, 1954, Maria documented each day at sea, the ports where they landed, and most notably their arrival to Honolulu, Hawaii on Sunday, July 4 at 6:00 a.m. They briefly visited family members, and were back at sea by 10:00 p.m. They landed in San Francisco five days later on July 9, and Washington, D.C., was another five days by train. Their son Max (page 122) was born in November that year. (Courtesy of the Cacas family.)

MAGSAYSAY - GARCIA DINNER AND BALL
GIVEN BY
"I AM FOR MAGSAYSAY" ASSOCIATION, INC.
WASHINGTON HOTEL, WASHINGTON, D.C.
NOVEMBER 28, 1953
CULLEN

When World War II broke out, Ramon Magsaysay (1907–1957) joined the 31st Infantry Division of the Philippine Army and became known for his leadership in an intense antiguerrilla campaign against the Hukbalahap guerillas, earning great respect for the Philippine Infantry. In 1948, Magsaysay was chosen by Philippine president Manuel Roxas to go to Washington, D.C., as chairman of the committee on guerrilla affairs to help secure passage of the Rogers Bill that would ensure benefits to Philippine veterans—benefits that were finally approved in 2009—60 years later (page 122). Pictured above, a dinner and ball sponsored by the I Am For Magsaysay Association, Inc., was held at the Washington Hotel on November 28, 1953. (Courtesy of Maria DePeralta Ferrara.)

In February 1945, a group of 12 D.C. Filipino American veterans, fresh out of World War II, banded together with Gen. Carlos Romulo to establish the Gen. Vicente Lim Post 5471 Veterans of Foreign Wars of the United States. General Lim, born in 1888 in Laguna, Philippines, was selected to attend the U.S. Military Academy in West Point, New York, where he graduated as the academy's first Filipino (class of 1914). When the Japanese attacked the Philippines at the start of World War II, General Lim assumed a field command of the 41st Division of the Philippine Army. His campaign disrupted the Japanese timetable of invading the Philippines, giving the Americans more time to defend the mainland. The Lim post grew from the 12 original members and continues to this day. Above, the early members celebrate on New Year's Eve, 1958 (pages 37 and 104). Pictured below, Cayetano Hernando Domingo (1905–1996) is sworn in as the VFW Chaplain in the late 1980s. Domingo, also shown in an earlier portrait below left, lived with the Sabino family in Glassmanor, Maryland (pages 20 and 86). (Courtesy of the Chinn and Sarmiento families.)

In segregated Washington, Filipinos were neither white nor African American, and for many of the settlers during the post–World War II era, it was not always clear where they could live, work, socialize, or send their children to school. Large banks with racist lending policies rejected Filipino mortgage applications, so many turned to small savings and loan institutions to finance their new, single-family homes. In the photograph above, Paul Balbuena and Basilio Pimentil pose with young Ricky Balbuena. Behind the men, Felixberta Quidangen (right) chats with Wanda Balbuena (left) in front of the Quidangen home on Chesapeake Street in southeast D.C. In the photograph below, Quidangen (pages 40 and 51) sits on the back porch of the same house. (Courtesy of the Sarmiento family.)

The 1950s were a time of economic and social growth for young families who successfully purchased their first homes after living in public or military housing. In the photograph above, Clavelina "Lee" Quidangen poses on her bicycle outside of the Bellevue Housing Project in Bolling Air Force Base, where her family lived in the late 1940s; the rent at Bellevue was $32 per month. Lee's father, Melchor (page 39), worked at the Navy Yard Gun Factory across the South Capitol Street Bridge. Lee attended Kramer Junior High School, also in Anacostia. Below, she poses for a school picture in the early 1950s. (Courtesy of Clavelina Quidangen Sarmiento.)

After arriving from their long trip by ocean liner in 1954 (page 72), Clemente and Maria Cacas took the train from California to Washington, D.C. They stayed with Moises and Monica Bautista, Clemente's longtime friends at their home in Suitland, Maryland. Eventually, they moved to a small apartment on Minnesota Avenue, SE (page 68), but with a baby on the way, it was time for a single family home. They chose Prince George's County, Maryland, suburb of Glassmanor, where many Filipinos lived. In October 1955, they purchased a brick home on Maury Avenue (page 86) for $11,000. Above, new father Clemente holds his firstborn son, Max (page 99), at their new home. The deed to the home (below) included real tax stamps that validated the real-estate transaction. (Courtesy of the Cacas family.)

Flora Corpuz (page 52) came to Washington from the Philippines in 1952. She lived with her father, Max Corpuz (1908–1984; also pictured on page 43), who was a retired navy man and former steward to Ernest King, a five-star fleet admiral. Max opened a restaurant on H Street in Chinatown during the 1950s. Flora, pictured here standing in front of their house located at 7066 Ninth Street SE, studied nursing at Catholic University. (Courtesy of Flora Corpuz Nivera.)

Leon Alcoy (page 45) traveled to the Philippines in 1947 and married Ana Puyot, cousin of Leona Puyot Sevilla (page 50). Leon recalled that he ate in Caucasian-only restaurants and rode freely on public buses. They bought a house on Sheridan Street, NW, which, in the 1950s was a Caucasian, upper-middle class neighborhood. (Photograph by and courtesy of Rita Cacas, 1993.)

Pedro Sarmiento's family came to Washington after his retirement as a captain from the U.S. Army. In 1958, they bought a home in Chevy Chase, Maryland, to be near their older sons Larry and Pedro, who were already living in D.C. Here family members pose in front of the house with a *parol*, a paper star that decorates Filipino homes at Christmas (pages 40 and 41). (Courtesy of the Sarmiento family.)

Caesar Alzona was affiliated with the Philippine Resident Commissioner's Office in the late 1950s and early 1960s. Here his daughter Esperanza Patricia (page 81) enjoys a snowy Washington winter in front of their Woodley Park home in the late 1950s. Their family portrait is on page 82. (Courtesy of the Alzona family.)

Esperanza Patrica Alzona (page 80) was born in 1957 at the National Naval Medical Center in Bethesda, Maryland. She is pictured here during her baptism at St. Thomas Apostle Church in Washington, D.C., held by her godfather Manuel Quezon Jr., son of the former Philippine president (page 43), and her godmother, Mimi Laurel, daughter of the Philippine vice president. (Courtesy of Gus Alzona.)

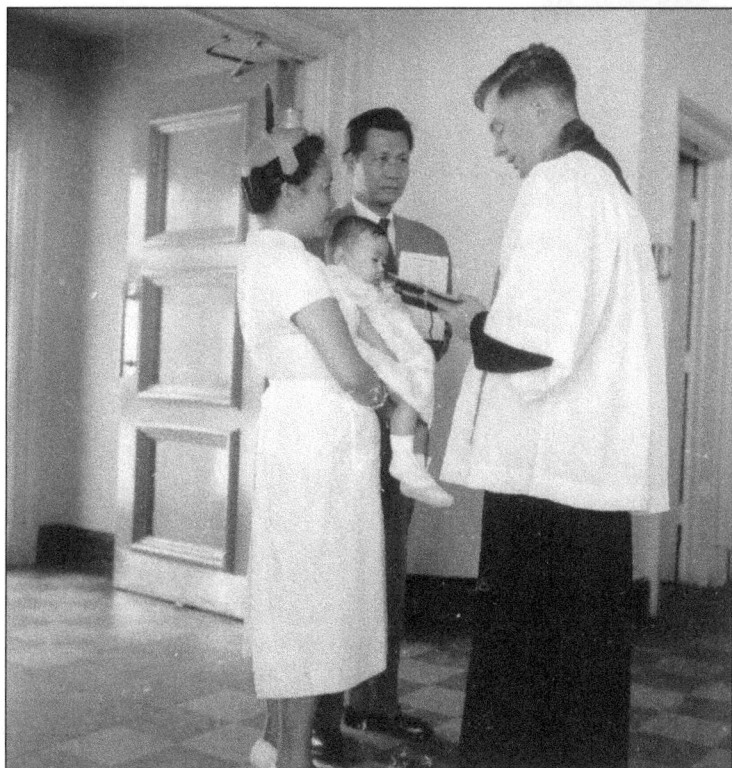

Rita Cacas, born in 1956 at the new Providence Hospital in Washington, D.C., was baptized at St. Thomas More Catholic Church by church pastor Fr. Raymond Fanning. Her godmother, Florentina DePeralta, had returned from France, where her husband, Alex, was stationed (page 54). They were to be Rita's godparents, but Alex was still in France, so Romulo Robles (center) stood in for him. (Courtesy of the Cacas family.)

After serving in World War II and the Korean War, and returning from France in 1949, Alex (b. 1915) and Florentina "Nena" (1918–2002) DePeralta (page 54) purchased their home on Observatory Place, in Northwest Washington, D.C. (page 89). Nena was a medical technician for the National Institutes of Health and retired in 1980. This was the family's Christmas card in the 1960s. (Courtesy of Maria DePeralta Ferrara.)

Caesar "Cesar" Alzona (1926–1997) from Laguna, Philippines, was a retired lawyer and former Philippine finance minister. He married Esperanza Cornejo (b. 1926), who was friends with President Quezon and Vice President Laurel. They were part of the close-knit Philippine government diplomatic corps living in D.C. during the 1950s and 1960s, and lived in Woodley Park (1957–1961) and Cleveland Park (1961–1963) in Northwest D.C. (Courtesy of Gus Alzona.)

Four

BUILDING THE CAPITAL BELTWAY

After more than a decade of planning and construction, the Capital Beltway opened in 1964, improving the flow of traffic and mobility for Washington-area residents and growing neighboring communities. The stretch of the beltway pictured above includes the main interchange near the Potomac River where D.C., Maryland, and Virginia meet, with a distant view of Maryland's Fort Washington and Oxon Hill communities, where many Filipinos settled. (Courtesy of the National Archives and Records Administration.)

Wash. D.C. 1959

The Interstate Highway System was established under Pres. Dwight Eisenhower in the 1950s. By the 1960s, automobiles were a necessity for many families in the United States. In the photograph above, Rafael "Larry" Sarmiento (page 92) poses by his family's cars in front of his parents' home off of Military Road, NW, in Chevy Chase, D.C. Pictured below, Clavelina "Lee" Sarmiento and her childhood friend Anita Karnes enjoy a summer afternoon in their neighborhood in the mid-1950s. (Courtesy of the Sarmiento family.)

Monica Selga (1909–1997), a schoolteacher in the Philippines for 25 years, came to D.C. in 1948, after her marriage to Moises Bautista (pages 25 and 46). Upon her arrival, she studied practical nursing and worked at the old Providence Hospital. In 1972, she retired from the Washington Hospital Center after 14 years. She is shown here at the National Mall during the 1960s. (Courtesy of the Cacas family.)

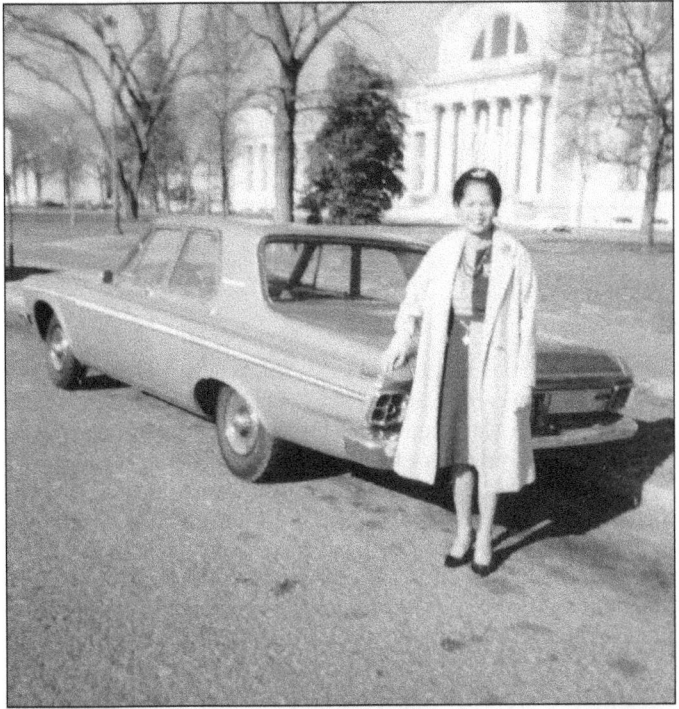

In 1945, Clemente Cacas (page 34) settled in D.C. and began his career driving a taxicab. He drove for the Bell Cab Association and bought his own taxicab in the 1960s under the Consolidated Cab Association, which exists today. He took one of his children with him in the taxi on Saturday mornings, telling them about places and social events that Filipinos enjoyed in Washington in the 1940s and 1950s. After 40 years of driving a cab, his family persuaded him to retire around 1980. (Courtesy of the Cacas family.)

The Glassmanor community attracted many Filipino families in the 1950s and 1960s. Maury Avenue is located on the Maryland side of D.C.'s Southern Avenue border, where there are affordable brick houses, and is convenient to the Eastover Shopping Center, St. Thomas More Catholic School and Church (page 88), grocery stores, a public library, and a bowling alley. Filipino families such as the Alamares, Buena, Cacas, Corpuz, Domingo, Fuñe, Guerrero, and Sabino families lived there from the late 1950s through the 1970s. Above, Israel "Danny" (1909–1978) and Felicidad "Fely" Guerrero (1928–1977) and their children pose for a family portrait in 1975. Pictured are Charles, Margie (page 88), Fely, Danny, and Rolondo. Danny (page 91) served in the U.S. Navy during World War II for 20 years, then continued as a civil servant for the Naval Research Lab for 24 years. In the photograph above right, Leonardo (b. 1922) and Filomena Fuñe (1929–2005) celebrate the graduation of their son Roy with daughter Kay. Leonardo was a photographer's mate in the U.S. Navy from 1945 until 1965, then became a professional photographer at the U.S. Department of Agriculture in Washington from 1965 until his retirement in 1979. Filomena was a dentist in the Philippines before she and Leonardo were married in 1955, then settled in Maryland. She worked as a central files supervisor, also at the USDA and was a member of the Vicente Lim VFW Post 5471 Ladies Auxiliary (page 104). (Courtesy of the Fuñe and Toribio families.)

Alfredo Sabino (page 18) stands proudly on his front porch on Dorchester Street (around the corner from Maury Avenue) on his way to his job as a security officer at the Naval Research Laboratory at Bolling Air Force Base. (Courtesy of Sandra Sabino Chinn.)

Luis Buena and his family originally lived near Hadley Hospital in southeast D.C., then moved to Glassmanor in the early 1960s. After the Bay of Pigs invasion in 1961, Buena wanted to send his family back to the Philippines, where they would be safe. This was their passport photograph, but the family never left D.C. Luis's wife, Teresa, is in the center, with their daughters Geraldine (left), Antoinette "Mary," and Loretta (front). They are pictured below during the late 1960s as young women. The community demographics changed during the 1970s and 1980s, as African American families moved out of D.C. and into the Prince George's County suburbs, and Filipinos bought larger homes in the nearby suburbs. Teresa was the last Filipino who lived on Maury Avenue (pages 39 and 53) until her death in 1995. (Courtesy of the Buena family.)

St. Thomas More Church and St. Thomas More School are located on Fourth Street, SE, in Washington, D.C., across the Maryland border, operated by the Franciscan Order of nuns and priests in the 1960s. St. Thomas More Church was the community church. Many Filipinos and other children from military families, who lived five miles away at Bolling Air Force Base, attended St. Thomas More School. Above, a demographically diverse group of six-year-old girls (from both private and public schools) gather after receiving the Catholic sacrament of First Holy Communion in 1962. Below, Maury Avenue Filipino children pose for portraits after their receiving First Holy Communion: left to right: Rita Cooper, and three Filipinas, Rita Cacas, Loretta "Lettie" Buena (page 87), and Margarita "Margie" Guerrero. The photograph on the right shows Roy and Kay Fuñe in 1963 (page 86). (Courtesy of the Cacas and Fuñe families.)

The Jelleff's Department Store, founded in 1910, was one of the upscale shopping institutions on Twelfth and F Streets NW—competing with S. Kanns Sons Co., The Hecht Company, Woodward & Lothrop, and Julius Garfinkel & Co. Jelleff's closed its doors in 1973. The store's founder, Frank Jelleff, also established D.C.'s first Boys and Girls Club, located at 3265 S Street, NW, and serving the Glover Park, Cleveland Park, and Woodley Park communities since the 1950s. Above, Alex DePeralta Jr. and his sister Maria Amorfina (center)—children of Alex and Florentina DePeralta (page 82)—participate in activities in the late 1950s. In 2009, due to financial problems and declining membership, the Boys and Girls Clubs of Greater Washington closed 22 clubs, including the oldest operating club, the Jelleff Branch. (Courtesy of Maria DePeralta Ferrara.)

The DePeralta and Cacas families rented gardening spaces in the Glover Park community, Victory Gardens on Tunlaw Road, NW, around the corner from the DePeralta home on Observatory Place, near the current residence of the U.S. vice president. Here daughters of Clemente and Maria Cacas (page 72), Rita (left) and Emily (b. 1958), pose for a picture in 1963, while their parents worked in the gardens. Emily received her bachelor's of science and master's of science in nursing from Georgetown University and has been a pediatric nurse at the Children's National Medical Center for over 30 years. (Courtesy of the Cacas family.)

Washington, D.C., in the early 1960s was still segregated. African Americans lived in designated places—in the southeast and southwest quadrants of Washington, and in southern Maryland counties across the Anacostia River. Whites lived in the northwest and northeast quadrants, and in northern and western Maryland and Virginia counties. Sandra Sabino Chinn, daughter of Alfredo Sabino (page 20), who grew up in Glassmanor, recalled signs at Chesapeake Beach in the 1940s warning, "No dogs, No Filipinos, No Jews." But Filipinos were welcomed in places like Chapel Point State Park in rural Calvert County about 25 miles away from Washington. Above, a group of Filipinos that included the Quidangen (page 76) and the Cabigas families enjoy a potato sack race at Chapel Point State Park. Filipinos enjoy a picnic (right), also at Chapel Point. (Courtesy of the Sarmiento and Toribio families.)

Filipinos in the 1950s and 1960s were part of the generation of baby boomers. The children of the pioneers and new immigrants continued their parents' goals of success and higher education. The second and third generations were groomed by their parents and their communities to live and be educated in the mainstream with service to family, community, church, and country. Above, Maury Avenue Filipinos Danny Guerrero (page 86) at the far left, and his wife, Fely—holding her son Rolondo—watch over children during a neighborhood picnic. Below, Gus Alzona (center with white suit and bow tie) celebrates his birthday with his siblings, Woodley Park neighborhood friends, and other relatives in 1958 (page 82). (Courtesy of the Toribio family and Gus Alzona.)

Rafael "Larry" Sarmiento (b. 1937) attended Washington College in Chestertown, Maryland, in 1961, earning a bachelor of science degree in chemistry. He continued studies in chemistry at the American University and earned a doctorate in chemistry in 1975. He is pictured above with his father, Pedro, his mother, Cresenciana, and his sister Helen (page 40). Larry became an accomplished organic chemist (specializing in pesticides) for the U.S. Department of Agriculture in Beltsville, Maryland, and participated in published USDA research; the photograph on the left is from the May 1973 issue of *Agricultural Research* magazine. Larry retired in 1995 after 30 years of federal government service. (Courtesy of the Sarmiento family.)

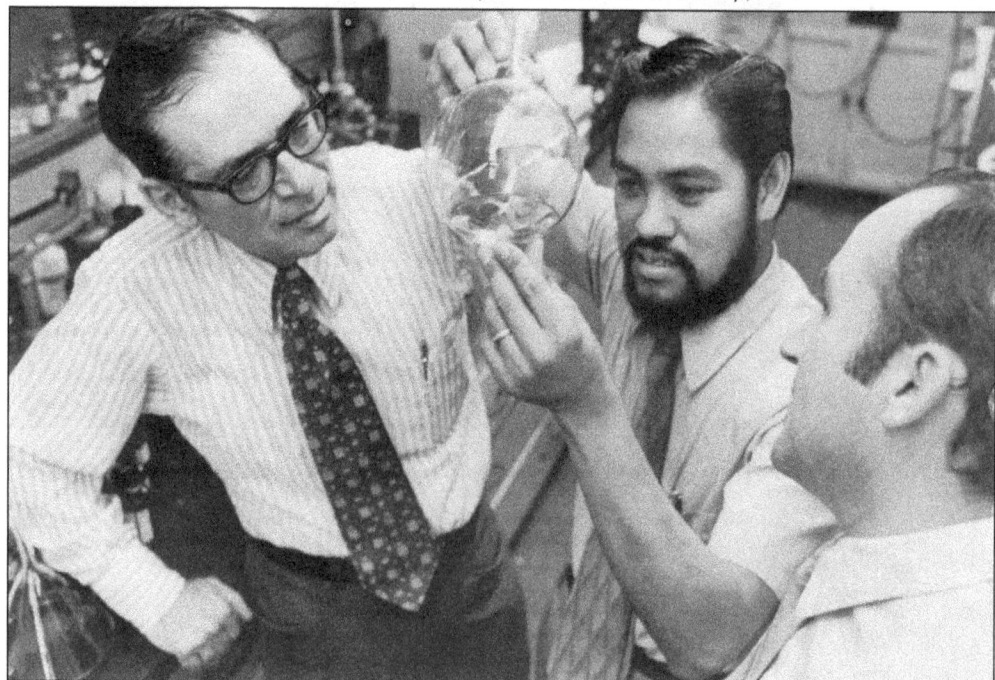

Josefino Cacas Comiso (b. 1940) came to the United States in 1962 after earning a bachelor of science degree in physics (University of the Philippines, 1962), a master's of science in physics (Florida State University, 1966), and a doctorate in physics (UCLA, 1972). He held a postdoctoral position at the University of Virginia (Charlottesville, 1973–1977). Josefino is the nephew of D.C. pioneer, Clemente Cacas (pages 25, 102, and 121). (Courtesy of the Cacas family.)

Roberto Lagdameo (b. 1946) came to the United States in 1963 and studied accounting at Benjamin Franklin University. Fe Palting (b. 1944) arrived in 1966, after touring Europe. She applied for a visa at the U.S. embassy as a systems analyst, and then National Cash Register hired her as a computer programmer. The two met in D.C. and, three months later, were married in 1975. Their story continues on page 101. (Courtesy of the Lagdameo family.)

During the 1960s, the increased desire for population growth and diversity created major policy reforms in immigration laws, which dropped exclusionary country quotas. These reforms resulted in increasing the number of immigrants from Asia and the Pacific regions, including the Philippines. A new generation of Filipinos arrived in the mid- to late 1960s, some of whom had ties with the early pioneers. Sponsored by her sister Maria Cacas (page 57), Lourdes Bello (front, fourth from the right) came to the United States in 1969. Her family and relatives said goodbye at this farewell *despedida* at the Manila airport, on her journey to America. (Courtesy of the Cacas family.)

Five

BEYOND THE BELTWAY

From the 1970s to the 1990s, the Filipino community expanded along with that of the greater Washington, D.C., community. The pioneer families branched out beyond the beltway. Their children and grandchildren continued their parents' early trend toward greater multicultural, biracial, interracial, and blended families. These U.S.-born generations were active in the civic life of D.C., but continued to move to outer suburbs and rural Virginia and Maryland. Here a Filipino youth group performs on the Capitol grounds (Courtesy of the Fuñe family.)

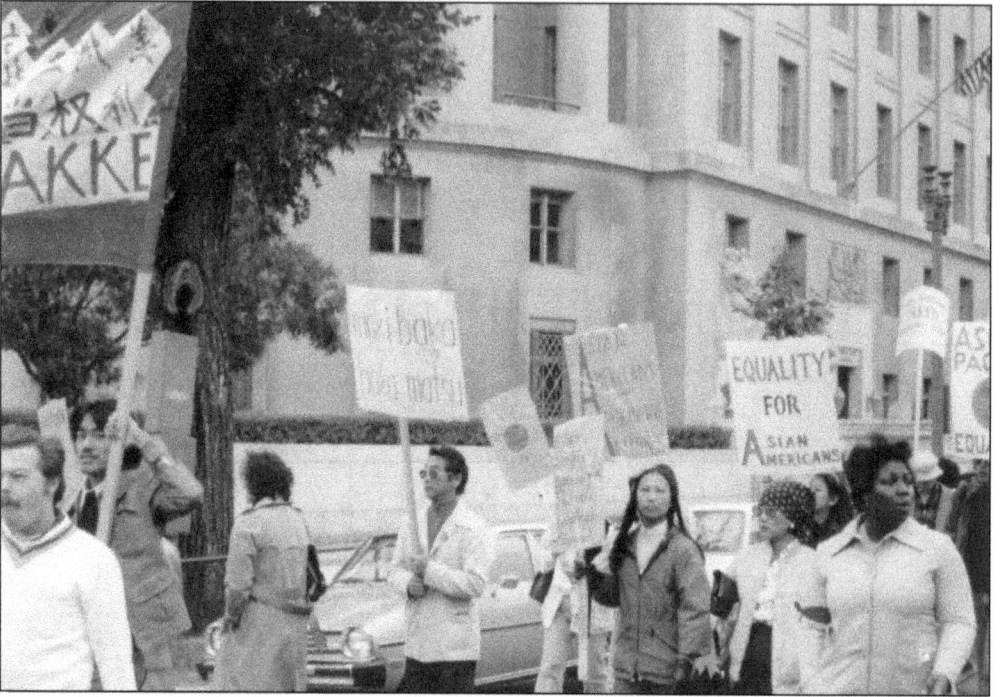

Juanita Tamayo (b. 1948) came to Washington, D.C., in 1973 from San Francisco via Chicago. Her parents, Lazaro Tamayo and Anicia Lucas, were pioneer leaders in San Francisco's Filipino community. Her dad was a founding member and officer of the International Family Circle in 1939 that focused on San Francisco electoral politics and labor rights. He was also a member of the 1930s Filipino Aviators Club. In 1973, Juanita married fellow University of Chicago graduate Robert Henry Lott (1948–2008), a second-generation Washingtonian born in old Providence Hospital. Their third-generation Washingtonian sons, David Tamayo Lott and Joseph Henry Lott III, were born at the Washington Hospital Center and graduated from the Computer, Math, and Science Magnet Program at Montgomery Blair High School and the University of Maryland, College Park. Above, Juanita, in the center with a dark jacket, marches for Asian American equality in front of the U.S. Department of Justice to protest the 1978 historic affirmative action Supreme Court decision *Regents of the University of California v. Bakke*. With her is another social justice activist, Sam Cacas (page 101), carrying a large sign at the far left. The photograph below was the 2006 Lott family Christmas photograph. (Courtesy of Juanita Tamayo Lott.)

Rita Cacas's parents sent her (and later, sister Emily, page 89) to the Academy of Notre Dame (1970–1974), a women's inner city high school in D.C., next to Gonzaga High School, which her brothers Max and Sam attended. Around 1970, the school went from predominantly white to predominantly black. As one of two Filipinos in the school at that time, Rita became deeply exposed to multicultural and multiracial issues, including black power, the American Indian movement, anti–Vietnam War protests, and feminist studies. After her graduation in 1974, Rita and Sam (page 101) marched in minority and women's rights demonstrations. They attended the University of Maryland, College Park in the late1970s; took American Studies classes; and dreamed of a curriculum about Filipino history. (Courtesy of the Cacas family.)

Walter Washington was the first elected mayor of the District of Columbia and served from 1975 until 1979. Anthony "Tony" Sarmiento, son of pioneers Pedro and Cresenciana (page 40), became engaged in civic activities during the 1970s and worked in Mayor Washington's Youth Office, then became a leader in union, education, and senior services (page 120). Below, Florentina DePeralta (page 82) poses with Mayor Washington; she was also very active in local and national civic organizations. (Courtesy of the Sarmiento family, and Maria DePeralta Ferrara.)

Max Cacas (b. 1954), son of pioneers Clemente and Maria Cacas (page 72), was born in the old Providence Hospital and attended Gonzaga College High School. Max is a veteran broadcast/online journalist, with over 30 years of news experience with local commercial and public radio stations, and national broadcast networks (NPR, CBS, ABC). He is currently a reporter with WFED and WTOP Radio in Washington, D.C. (Courtesy of WFED/WTOP Radio.)

Founded in 1982, the Filipino American National Historical Society (FANHS) promotes the understanding, education, enlightenment, appreciation, and enrichment through the identification, gathering, preservation, and dissemination of the history and culture of Filipino Americans in the United States. The FANHS national office and archives is located in Seattle, Washington, and supports 27 chapters, including East Coast chapters in Hampton Roads (Virginia), Metropolitan New York, New England, and Pennsylvania. Above, the FANHS Pennsylvania chapter gathers to celebrate Filipino American History Month in October 2008. Photographed from left to right are (sitting) Robert and Juanita Tamayo Lott; (standing) three unidentified, Joan May Cordova, and two unidentified. (Courtesy of Joan May Cordova.)

Mencie Martires Yaguil (b. 1949) and Ernest Hairston (b. 1939) met at Gallaudet University in Washington, D.C., in 1976 where she was doing graduate work in education for the hearing impaired and he was a guest lecturer in her class. Ernie was a member of the first integrated class at the West Virginia School for the Deaf in Romney, West Virginia, and among the first black students accepted at Gallaudet. They married in the Philippines in 1978 and then moved to Seabrook, Maryland, a black community with many highly educated professionals and known for its acceptance of multiracial children. They are longtime community leaders in Prince George's County and proud parents to Tal, Darlene, Mayumi, Malaya, and Tala, and proud grandparents to Yumi's daughter, Sofie Grace (page 117). (Courtesy of Mencie Hairston.)

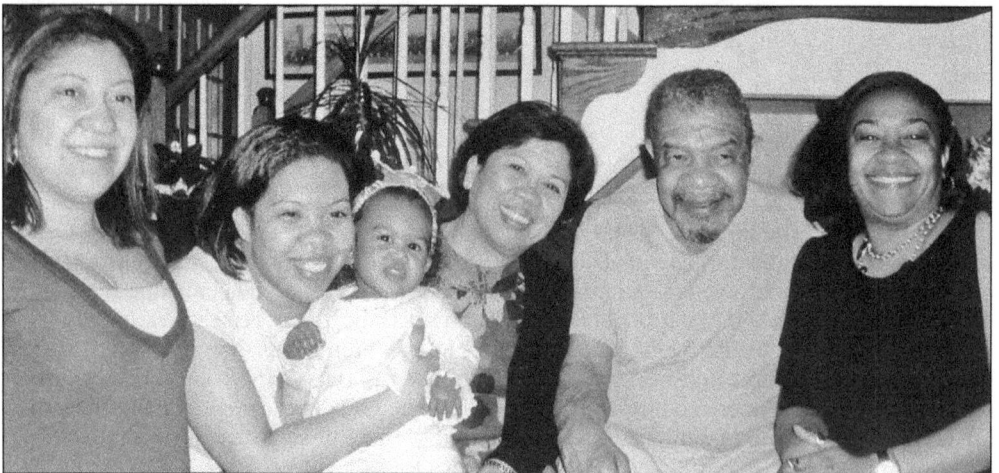

Samuel Cacas (b. 1955), son of Clemente and Maria Cacas (page 72), graduated from Archbishop Carroll High School in 1973, then attended Antioch Law School (now University of D.C. Law School). He married Dora Love in 2000. Sam is a San Francisco journalist and writer. His first novel, *BlAsian Exchanges* (2007), explores black and Asian voices that influenced his life growing up during the 1960s and 1970s. See also pages 96 and 97. (Photograph by and courtesy of Lina Undayag McDowell, 2008.)

Lina Undayag McDowell is the daughter of Moises (1937–2008) and Lourdes Undayag (page 94), who have lived in Adelphi, Maryland since 1972. Lina attended Central High School in Prince George's County, Maryland. She married Steven McDowell in 2002, and their son Steven Jr. was born in 2006. Here all three are wearing traditional formal Filipino dress called *barongs*. (Courtesy of Lina Undayag McDowell.)

Fe and Roberto Lagdameo were married at St. Thomas More Church in Arlington, Virginia, in 1975. Principal sponsors included Philippine ambassador Ernesto Lagdameo Sr., Roberto's uncle. At this time, Roberto was a data programmer for National Cash Register in Washington, and Fe was an auditor for a CPA firm in Washington, D.C. This 1984 portrait shows their five children, Roberto Jr., Christina, Ricardo, Angela, and Rodrigo (pages 93 and 116). (Courtesy of the Lagdameo family.)

Josefino Comiso (page 90) married Diana Jimenez in 1970. Diana received her master of science degree in nursing from Georgetown University (1988), and retired after 15 years as nursing director for two major nursing facilities in the Washington area. She is currently a clinical instructor at Howard Community College (pages 94 and 119). (Courtesy of the Cacas family.)

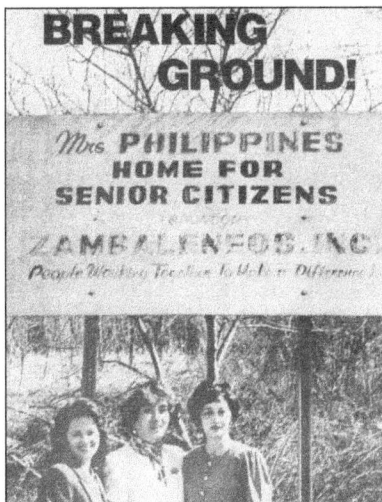

Napoleon Lechoco (b. 1930), came to the United States in 1958 to attend a conference and returned in 1972 when his wife, Leticia, came to work for Philippine president Ferdinand Marcos's wife, Imelda. In 1983, they held a party at their Birchwood City home in Oxon Hill, Maryland, and formed a group called the Zambaleneos of Metropolitan, D.C., which sought to build a senior citizens center. The Mrs. Philippines Home for Senior Citizens, Inc., became a nonprofit organization eligible for government funding through the U.S. Department of Housing and Urban Development and in 1990 received $3,525,000 to purchase land and build a 74-unit facility in Oxon Hill. The home has served as a community meeting place for a variety of local organizations, including the monthly assembly of the Vicente Lim Post 5471 Veterans of Foreign Wars of the U.S. and Ladies Auxiliary (page 104). Lechoco was active in local civic activities, including the Prince George's County Parks and Planning Commission. (Photographs by Rita Cacas, 2009; courtesy of Napoleon Lechoco.)

The pioneers and their families continue to thrive in their civic organizations, especially related to military service such as the Vicente Lim Post 5471 VFW (page 75). The Ladies Auxiliary was added in 1954, the Sons of VFW in 1968, and Junior Girls Unit in 1970. Their community and humanitarian projects include support for the VFW National Home for widows and orphans of veterans; Veterans Buddy Poppy (Cancer Research) Program; bingo nights; Thanksgiving Day events to boost the morale of veterans at the VA Hospital; visits to the D.C. Village (page 53) for handicapped youth and senior citizens; provision of food to Mother Teresa's House and Carmelite sisters for homeless women; and promotion of patriotism. The picture above shows past VFW commanders. Below left, members of the Association of Philippine American Women (APAW) gather for a portrait in 1968. APAW member Cresenciana Sarmiento (page 40) at the far left, was very active in civic, gardening, and neighborhood organizations. Prince George's County journalist Hilariona Piñera (1920–2003) is seated in the middle. Below right, the Ladies Auxiliary gathers in 2004. (Photograph below right by Rita Cacas, 2004; courtesy of the Sarmiento family.)

Beauty pageants, common in their Philippine homeland, appeared in the late 1960s and continue within Oxon Hill and Fort Washington, Maryland, communities associated with the post-1965 immigrants. Here the winner of the Miss Philippine Community title proudly wears her crown at pre–Fourth of July celebrations sponsored by the Benevolent Association of Washington, held at the Presidential Arms Hotel in Washington, D.C., on July 2, 1966. As the population of Filipinos grew in the 1990s, churches such as St. Ignatius Church and St. Columba Catholic Church (both in Oxon Hill, Maryland), St. Michael the Archangel Church (Silver Spring, Maryland), St. Rose of Lima Catholic Church (Gaithersburg, Maryland), and St. Bernadette Parish (Springfield, Virginia) offered Sunday Mass in the Pilipino language. Below is a portrait of an all-Filipino choir that performs for the St. Columba congregation. (Courtesy of the Fuñe family.)

Violeta "Belen" De La Peña was born in 1932 in Malasiqui, Philippines, and came to the United States in 1955. Her husband, Remo, was a retired U.S. sailor, employed by the U.S. Bureau of Naval Personnel when they moved to D.C. in 1962. They settled in Fort Washington in the early 1970s. Belen studied computer programming in the early 1960s, worked at George Washington University and Georgetown Hospital, setting up their first computer operations in the late 1960s. Her first government job was with the Office of Economic Opportunity, created during Pres. Lyndon Johnson's War on Poverty and terminated under Pres. Richard Nixon. Unable to have children, Belen has devoted most of her life to enhancing the quality of life for Filipino Americans, fostering pride in their cultural heritage—with a particular concern for children. Working with her immediate community, she has been a mentor in recognizing talent and potential in children. Around 1980, she founded the Pilipino American Cultural Arts Society, or PACAS—a formal Filipino performing folk dance troupe in the Washington area. Below, PACAS dancers display traditional Filipino performances. Belen was also one of the founding members of the Maryland Asian Pacific American Council. She was recognized in a 1994 publication, *Women of Achievement in Prince George's County History* by Therese Yewell, published by the Maryland-National Park and Planning Commission. (Courtesy of Belen De La Peña.)

Teresa Ferrara (b. 1990), center, is the daughter of Dennis and Maria (page 89) DePeralta Ferrara, left; and granddaughter of pioneers Alex and Florentina DePeralta (page 82). She graduated salutatorian (and outstanding vocalist) from the Duke Ellington School of the Arts in 2008 and is studying vocal performance at the University of Maryland School of Music. Already an exceptional 18-year-old, Teresa prepares for an opera career. (Photograph by and courtesy of Rita Cacas, 1993.)

Augustus Caesar "Gus" Alzona (b. 1952), born in Pasay City, Philippines, came to D.C. with his family in the late 1950s (page 82). Gus is a longtime Filipino American community volunteer and political activist. He was elected 2006–2010 Republican Party central committee member (Maryland Legislative District 16) and is also a musician. In this photograph, Gus performs with his band, Trademark, during Fiesta Asia 2008. (Courtesy of Gus Alzona.)

Many artistic communities developed during the 1980s, and the artistic talents and contributions of the Filipino community were recognized through exhibits and organizations showcasing multiple generations of Filipino artists, often sponsored by the Philippine Embassy or the World Bank. The Philippine Art, Letters, and Media (PALM) Council, sponsors literary readings, Philippine education, and cultural lectures by prominent scholars and poets. Group art exhibitions, such as the one pictured above held at the Philippine Embassy, included Washington artists Rita Cacas (daughter of Clemente Cacas) and Joey Manlapaz (niece of Evangline Paredes). Below, a 2002 exhibit was held at the Martin Luther King Library entitled "Brown Strokes on a White Canvas," organized by Virginia artist, Julian Oteyza, and including Philippine artists Nilo Santiago, Frank Redondo, Maria Davidoff, and Marvin Santos. (Photographs by Christopher Cook, 2002 and 2004.)

In 2006, the Smithsonian Institution commemorated "100 Years of Filipinos in the U.S." with public programs and a traveling exhibit chronicling Filipino American history. Pictured are members of the planning committee: (first row) Gina Inocencio, Jon Melegrito, Noel Izon, and Franklin Odo (director, Smithsonian Institution Asian Pacific American Program); (second row, standing) Joy Quintana, Francey Youngberg, Tito Tolentino, Juanita Tamayo Lott, Gloria Caoile, Irene Bueno, Bing Branigan, Maurese Oteyza Owens, Michael Chupeco, Mary Anne Fadul, and Jojo Maralit. (Courtesy of the Asian Pacific American Program, Smithsonian Institution.)

Maj. Gen. Antonio Mario Taguba (b. 1950), born in the Philippines and raised in Hawaii, is retired from the U.S. Army. He was featured at the third Smithsonian Filipino American Centennial Commemoration program in 2006 entitled "A salute to Filipino American Men and Women in the U.S. Military." He authored *The Taguba Report*, an internal U.S. Army report on detainee abuse at Abu Ghraib prison in Iraq, published in 2004. Recognized worldwide for his courage and patriotism, General Taguba is a genuine American hero and role model. His only son is currently serving in the U.S. Army in the Middle East. (Courtesy of Maj. Gen. Antonio Taguba.)

Pioneers Clemente and Maria Cacas (page 72), center, sitting, are shown here with four generations representing their extended D.C. families: the Bello family, the Undayag and Comiso families (page 102), the Gonzales, Cacas Myers, and the Cacas Cook families gathering for a Christmas portrait at the house of Emily (page 89) and Nilo Gonzales. In the front are Rita Cacas and her husband, Christopher Cook, sitting on the right. Chris is also a photographer who has followed Rita around with his camera to numerous family and Filipino American events, taking many of the photographs in this book. (Courtesy of the Cacas family.)

Remegio Cabacar (b. 1927), joined the U.S. Navy at age 17, served in World War II and the Korean War, and retired after 25 years. He arrived in Washington, D.C., in 1960, beginning a second career with the FBI, and retired after 15 years of federal service. The Cabacars were among the founding members of the Zambaleneos of Metropolitan Washington, D.C. (page 103). Cabacar is pictured here (center, holding his grandson) with his wife, Carolina (who also worked at the FBI), and their extended family in 2008. (Courtesy of the Cabacar family.)

The Toribio family's century of presence in the Washington area has now branched into its fourth generation. This 1996 portrait shows family pioneer Fermina Santos Peji (page 14), left, who came to the United States in 1915; her niece Amparing (center) and Leo Toribio; Amparing's daughter Nila (page 124) on the left, and husband, Joe Straka, with their son Kiel. Fermina (pictured age 86) was a successful restaurateur for over 50 years (page 63) and was being cared for by the Toribios. She returned to the Philippines in 1996, where she passed away. The 2006 portrait below is an incomplete group of the extended family. Family members are scattered in the Washington area, and around the country. (Photographs by and courtesy of Christopher Cook, 1996 and 2006.)

Formed around 1978 to unite other Filipinos and increase awareness of the Filipino culture through academic, athletic, and social programs, the Filipino Cultural Association (FCA) at University of Maryland, College Park (UMCP), was formally established in 1981. It was one of the first Filipino American student associations in the metropolitan Washington area. For 25 years, FCA has hosted the annual spring Philippine Culture Night, featuring local talent, dance troupes, stage performances, and fashion events. FCA is also a founding member-organization of the Filipino

Intercollegiate Networking Dialogue (FIND) and is the sixth of seven East Coast districts, comprising participation by colleges and universities from Washington, D.C. (Catholic University of America, American, George Washington, and Georgetown Universities); Maryland (UMCP, University of Maryland at Baltimore, Loyola College, the U.S. Naval Academy, and occasionally Montgomery College); and Virginia (George Mason University). (Courtesy of Matt Sinkiat.)

In 2006, a few adult children of the Washington, D.C., pioneers began sharing stories of growing up prior to the Capital Beltway, calling themselves Before the Beltway. They discussed how the repeal of antimiscegenation laws legalized mixed-race marriages, making it easier for the next generation; they described changing neighborhood demographics resulting from race riots in the late 1960s; and they lamented preliminary survey data about Filipino American schoolchildren who are not faring as well as their older brothers and sisters. Strategically they partnered with the University of Maryland's Filipino Cultural Association to analyze these trends through formal leadership, mentoring, and scholarship programs. Pictured here are four of the group's leaders, Lisa Chinn, Juanita Tamayo Lott, Sandy Sabino Chinn, and Rita Cacas. Sandy and Lisa are the daughter and granddaughter, respectively, of D.C. pioneer Alfredo Sabino (page 20). Sandy Chinn directed the Human Relations Department of Prince George's County Public Schools in the 1980s and 1990s. Lisa is a researcher and reporter for ABC's *The World News with Charles Gibson*. She received the Peabody and Dupont Awards in broadcast journalism for her research on coverage during September 11, 2001. (Photograph by Christopher Cook, 2006..)

Six

GLOBAL LEADERS FOR THE 21ST CENTURY

Filipino leaders in Washington, D.C., today are a cumulative body of education, knowledge, networks, sacrifice, courage, and compassion. Inside Washington and beyond the beltway, they work together in diverse coalitions to ensure American heritage for the next generations. Above are some founding contributors for the Major General Antonio Taguba Profiles in Courage and Leadership Scholarship, Asian American Studies (AAST) at the University of Maryland, College Park. Pictured are Steve Encomienda, Ryan Herrera, Juanita Tamayo Lott, Jonathan Sterlin, Mencie Hairston, General Taguba, Pete Sarmiento, Richard Hawks, Betty Lee Hawks, Larry Shinagawa (Director, AAST at UMCP), Tony Sarmiento, Lee Quidangen Sarmiento, Vangie Paredes, Rita Cacas, Donna Hamilton (associate provost for Academic Affairs and dean of Undergraduate Studies, UMCP), and Kris Valderrama. There are names, faces, and stories that did not make it onto the pages of this book—but this book is just a beginning. The rich history of East Coast Filipinos is ready to be told. (Photograph by and courtesy of Christopher Cook, 2009.)

David Valderrama and his daughter Kriselda "Kris" Valderrama are examples of intergenerational electoral leaders. Each was elected to the Maryland House of Delegates, representing Prince George's County District 26. From 1985 until 1990, David was a judge for the Prince George's County Orphan's Court, then from 1991 until 2003 became the first Filipino American elected to the Maryland Legislature. Since 2006, he has served on the Prince George's County Economic Development Corporation. Kris is the current District 26 delegate, elected in 2007. She is a member of the Judiciary Committee and Women Legislators of Maryland. A Washingtonian and graduate of Oxon Hill High School and Salisbury State University, Kris is a member of St. Columba Church (page 106). Kris is pictured below addressing attendees at the 2009 FCA and FAST Gala (page 119), where her two daughters joined her on the stage. (Above photograph, courtesy of the Fuñe family; below photograph by Christopher Cook, 2009.)

Young adults display leadership by service in a range of volunteer activities on campus, in the workplace, and in the community. A prominent example that relies on student volunteers is Camp Mabuhay (based in Prince George's County), started in 1996 with American mothers of adopted Filipino children, the Philippine Embassy, and Mencie Hairston (page 100), pictured here of the Mabuhay Culture School of Maryland. Below, children participate in Camp Mabuhay activities in 2006. (Above photograph, by and courtesy of Christopher Cook, 2009; below photograph, courtesy of Mencie Hairston.)

The first Filipino American Studies (FAST) at the University of Maryland, College Park (UMCP) was established in 2007 from the work of Asian American Studies (AAST) director Dr. Larry Shinegawa, the Filipino Cultural Association (FCA), and Before the Beltway (page 114). The FCA and AAST sponsored the first annual FAST Gala in 2007 to inaugurate FAST and to raise funds for its scholarship fund. Two awards were presented to D.C. pioneer Evangeline Paredes and to Christina Lagdameo for her pioneering efforts to establish an AAST Program. The photograph above is from the 2007 inaugural gala. Pictured are Maricel Hernandez (FCA president, 2007–2008), Maria and Rita Cacas, Vangie Paredes, and Ryan Herrera (FCA president, 2005–2006). The photograph below shows Christina and Angela Lagdameo (page 102). Christina advocated for AAST as president of the Asian American Student Union in 1997. With other UMCP student leaders, she successfully persuaded the university to establish an AAS program. Angela became the first Filipina student body president of UMCP in 2001. (Above photograph, courtesy of Matt Sinkiat; below photograph, courtesy of the Lagdameo family.)

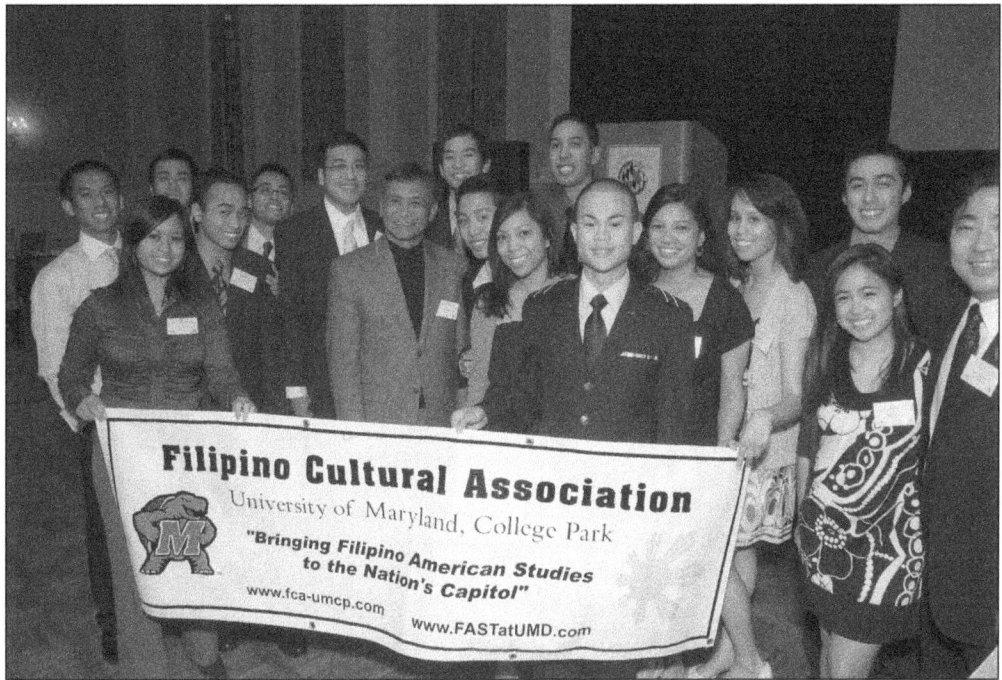

The Filipino Cultural Association (FCA, page 113), founded in 1978 at the University of Maryland, College Park, was instrumental in developing Filipino American Studies (FAST) in 2007 under 2006–2007 president Jonathan Sterlin and vice president Ryan Herrera. The above photograph was taken on the historical launch of the Major General Antonio Taguba Profiles in Courage and Leadership Scholarship by the Filipino Cultural Assocation (page 125) and Filipino American Studies (FAST) Asian American Studies, University of Maryland, College Park on February 21, 2009, in the grand ballroom at the Adele Stamp Student Union. Pictured below are Jonathan Sterlin, Pedro Sarmiento, General Taguba, and Ryan Herrera. (Photographs by and courtesy of Christopher Cook, 2009.)

Gem Daus (b. 1966) was born in Baguio, Philippines, grew up in Norfolk, Virginia, and graduated from the University of Virginia. He is the first Filipino American Studies professor for the Asian American Studies Program at the University of Maryland, College Park (page 118). Daus is also a health policy and organization development consultant. He was honored in 2003 as a health care hero by the Congressional Black, Hispanic, Native American, and Asian and Pacific American Caucuses. From 2000 to 2007, he staffed the Washington, D.C., office of the Asian and Pacific Islander American Health Forum (Courtesy of Gem Daus.)

The Organization of Young Filipino Americans (OYFA) at the University of Virginia, established in 1988, includes many Filipinos and non-Filipinos from the Washington area. The group promotes Filipino culture in Charlottesville, Virginia. In 2008, OYFA celebrated their 20th anniversary, inviting Rita Cacas (second row, second from the right) to give her presentation about Washington, D.C., Filipino pioneers (page 125). (Photograph by Christopher Cook, 2008.)

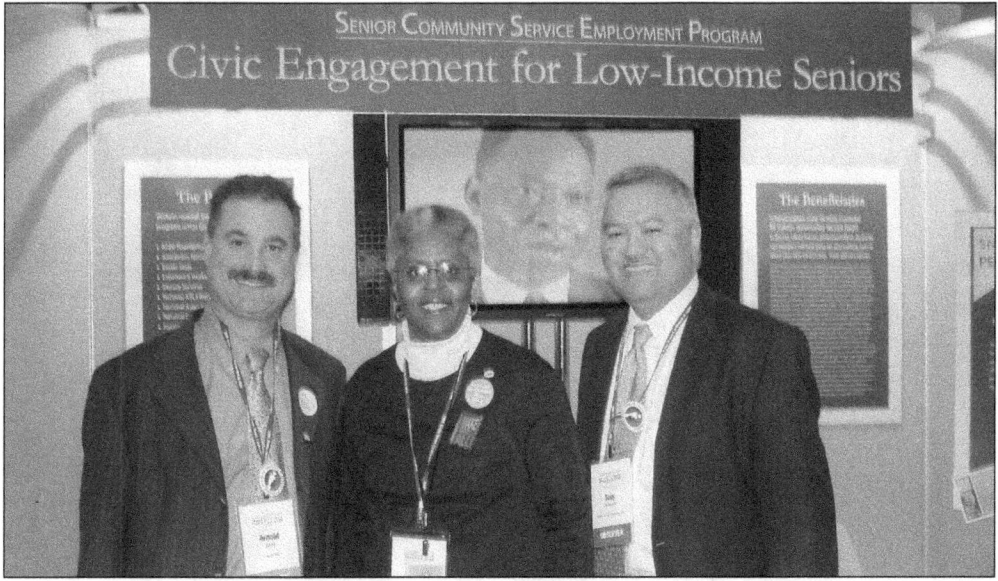

Anthony "Tony" Sarmiento (b. 1951) is the son of Washington pioneers Pedro and Crescenciana Sarmiento (page 40) and has a long history of civic service to local and national leaders and organizations. After working on youth programs for the D.C. government under Mayor Walter Washington (page 98), Tony joined the staff of the AFL-CIO, the national federation of labor unions in 1979. In recognition of his expertise in adult education and worker training, Pres. Bill Clinton appointed him to the board of the National Institute for Literacy in 1996. In 2000, he was appointed executive director of Senior Service America, Inc., a national nonprofit organization that assists low-income older adults in rejoining the labor force. In the photograph above, taken in 2005, Tony poses with two delegates from Senior Service America, Inc., sub-grantee organizations. In the photograph below, Tony chats with Maryland governor Martin O'Malley during a break at the 2008 Maryland Governor's Workforce Summit, where he was one of the panelists. (Courtesy of Tony Sarmiento.)

Josefino Cacas Comiso (page 90) has enjoyed a distinguished federal career spanning over 30 years as a senior scientist at NASA's Goddard Space Flight Center. Josefino was the chief scientist for many NASA missions in Arctic and Antarctic field programs, specializing in satellite-observed climate change research in the polar regions. He was a contributing author to the 2007 Intergovernmental Panel on Climate Change (IPCC) report that was awarded half of a 1997 Nobel Peace Prize—the other half went to former vice president Al Gore. Above, Josefino was honored at the 20 Outstanding Filipino Americans event held by *Filipino Image* magazine in 2002. Pictured are daughter Melissa Comiso Pope, son Glenn Comiso, Josefino Comiso, cousin Rita Cacas, son David Comiso, aunt Maria Cacas, sister Patria Comiso, and cousin Emily Cacas Gonzales (pages 87, 90, and 98). (Above photograph, by and courtesy of Christopher Cook; Below photograph, courtesy of the Comiso family.)

Networking within D.C.-area Asian Pacific Americans organizations for over 10 years, Ben de Guzman's leadership as national coordinator for the National Alliance for Filipino Veterans Equity led to the successful passage of the Filipino World War II veterans legislation in 2009, providing official recognition and financial support. The NAFVE members gathered here are (first row) Charmaine Manansala, Irene Bueno, Rep. Mike Honda (D-CA); (second row) Ben, Vida Benavides, Lillian Galedo, and Jon Melegrito (page 72). (Photograph by Bing Branigin, 2009.)

Joan May "Joanie" Timtiman Cordova is an associate teaching professor of education and director of Drexel University's Multicultural Collaborative in Philadelphia, Pennsylvania. She received a merit-based fellowship from Harvard University, where she received her doctorate degree, focusing her research on educational experiences of second-generation Filipinos. Joanie is also national president of the Filipino American National Historical Society (page 99). (Courtesy of Joan May Cordova.)

Following in the footsteps of her maternal grandmother, Asuncion Gaudiel (page 64), Leonila "Nila" Toribio Straka (page 66), the daughter of pioneers Amparing and Leo Toribio (pages 17 and 38) is now considered the *manang* of the Toribio family, providing a gathering place on Cobb Island, Maryland, for extended family and friends. A former head coach for volleyball at Georgetown University and Charles County Community College, she is currently active with the Side-Out Foundation and Dig Pink breast cancer organizations. Nila, a breast cancer survivor, poses with Michelle Obama at a White House event that featured the two organizations. (Courtesy of Nila Toribio.)

Sonia Aranza (b. 1961), pictured on the left, is a leader in the field of communications. Born in the Philippines, she came to the United States at the age of eight, immersed in the Filipino life of Hawaii. She married Filipino attorney Danny Aranza (b. 1960) in Hawaii in 1991. In 1991, they moved to Capitol Hill, where she worked for Congressman Neil Abercrombie (D-Hawaii) as director of Constituent Relations (1991–1997). Danny served in Pres. Bill Clinton's administration as director of Territorial and International Affairs. An award-winning speaker, Sonia was included in a listing of the "100 Most Influential Filipina-Americans in the U.S." Her parents passed to her the gift of Filipino heritage, and she has given her son the same passion. Aaron (b. 1994), pictured with Pres. Barack Obama, is a Virginia native with an appreciation for his Filipino roots. Aaron attends the Mabuhay Cultural School and dances traditional Filipino folk performances to equip him with enriching experiences for his future. (Courtesy of the Aranza family.)

Rita Cacas works at the National Archives and Records Administration and represents the Electronic Records Archives program, explaining the importance of preserving U.S. federal government records created today to ensure access by future generations. A native Washingtonian, her interest in the D.C. pioneers emerged in the 1980s, while interviewing her father, Clemente Cacas (page 25). She learned of the vibrant community of Filipinos whose stories, outside of their families, were unknown. Her 1993 project, *A Visit with My Elders: Portraits and Stories of Washington D.C. Filipino Pioneers,* documented these faces and stories. Above, Clemente attended the exhibition's opening reception at George Washington University in July 1994 (page 45). He passed away in 1995, and would have turned 100 years old in 2010—as this book is being released—a humbling celebration of the pioneers. Honoring our past leads us to the present and beyond. (Photographs by Christopher Cook, 1994, 2006, and 2009.)

While Juanita grew up in San Francisco, her entire adulthood has been spent in the Washington area. A retired federal senior demographer and policy analyst, she authored *Knowledge and Access: A Study of Asian and Pacific American Communities in the Washington, D.C. Metropolitan Area* (1989), *Asian Americans: From Racial Category to Multiple Identities* (1998), and *Common Destiny: Filipino American Generations* (2006). She cofounded the first Filipino American Studies program in the United States in 1969 at San Francisco State College and the Filipino American Studies at the University of Maryland, College Park in 2007. In preparation for the 2000 census, she was special assistant to the director of the U.S. Census Bureau, Martha Farnsworth Riche, pictured in the front left. (Above photograph by and courtesy of Christopher Cook, 2009; below photograph, courtesy of Juanita Tamayo Lott.)

BIBLIOGRAPHY

Alamar, Estrella Ravelo, and Willi Red Buhay. Images of America: *Filipinos in Chicago*. Charleston, SC: Arcadia Publishing, 2001.

Buell, Evangeline C., et al. Images of America: *Filipinos in the East Bay*. Charleston, SC: Arcadia Publishing, 2008.

Conroy, Sarah Booth. "Footsteps of the Filipino Pioneers." *The Washington Post* (July 25, 1994): 3.

George Washington University. *Filipinos and the American Dream, 1900–1945*. Washington, D.C.: The George Washington University, Colonnade Gallery, July 5–August 14, 1994.

Ibanez, Florante Peter, and Roselyn Estepa Ibanez. Images of America: *Filipinos in Carson and the South Bay*. Charleston, SC: Arcadia Publishing, 2009.

Japantown Task Force, Inc., The. Images of America: *San Francisco's Japantown*. Charleston, SC: Arcadia Publishing, 2005.

Lott, Juanita Tamayo. *Common Destiny, Filipino American Generations*. Lanham, MD: Rowman and Littlefield Publishing Group, Inc., 2006.

———. *Knowledge and Access: A Study of Asian and Pacific American Communities in the Washington, D.C. Area*. Washington, D.C.: Smithsonian Institution, 1989.

Mabalon, Dawn, et al. Images of America: *Filipinos in Stockton*. Charleston, SC: Arcadia Publishing, 2008.

Mondoñedo Smith, Nita. *Say Uncle! Life in DC with my Filipino Uncles*. Denver, CO: Outskirts Press, Inc., 2005.

———. *Forever in Our Hearts*. Baltimore, MD: Publish America, 2004.

Montoya, Carina Monica. Images of America: *Filipinos in Hollywood*. Charleston, SC: Arcadia Publishing, 2008.

National Archives and Records Administration. Photographs no. 54-14978 (page 10), SC-201178-5 (page 11), and, 306-PSD-54-1498, -1496 (page 26).

———. Record Group 350, *Bureau of Insular Affairs*, and Record Group 407, the *Philippine Archives Collection: Special List 61*. Washington, D.C.: National Archives and Records Administration (pages 10–12).

Orpilla, Mel. Images of America: *Filipinos in Vallejo*. Charleston, SC: Arcadia Publishing, 2005.

Visit us at
arcadiapublishing.com

www.ingramcontent.com/pod-product-compliance
Lightning Source LLC
Chambersburg PA
CBHW080630110426
42813CB00006B/1652